Collective Bargaining in Local Government

By Evelina Moulder

Public employees have been organized for many years. Sixty-two percent of local government employee unions have been in existence for more than 20 years, according to the results of a survey on labor-management relations conducted by the International City/County Management Association (ICMA) in 1999. Employee unions are formed primarily to advocate improved wages and benefits as well as working conditions such as shift length and breaks. Unions represent their members in collective bargaining negotiations. They often exert political power through lobbying and campaign support. Depending on the number of union employees who live and vote in a municipality, union members can affect election outcomes. When unions and management have a strong, effective working relationship in which both roles are appreciated, together they can accomplish much.

ICMA conducted a survey that gathered information about many aspects of this necessary and often complex relationship. This Special Data Issue covers the overall management of collective bargaining within the local government—who negotiates, contingency plans in the event of a work stoppage, management rights clauses, and employee grievances. Two companion Special Data Issues—*Resolving Labor-Management Disputes: Public Safety* and *Resolving Labor-Management Disputes: Public Works and Sanitation*—examine grievances filed and dispute resolutions for police and fire services and for public works and sanitation services over a five-year period.

Table 1   Survey Response

Classification	No. of cities[1] surveyed (A)	No. of cities responding	% of (A)
Total, all cities	2,881	1,401	49
Population group			
Over 1,000,000	10	5	50
500,000-1,000,000	17	7	41
250,000-499,999	37	20	54
100,000-249,999	140	89	64
50,000-99,999	351	189	54
25,000-49,999	681	327	48
10,000-24,999	1,645	764	46
Geographic region			
Northeast	798	250	31
North-Central	811	400	49
South	735	423	58
West	537	328	61
Geographic division[2]			
New England	328	100	31
Mid-Atlantic	470	150	32
East North-Central	585	268	46
West North-Central	226	132	58
South Atlantic	318	203	64
East South-Central	150	68	45
West South-Central	267	152	57
Mountain	130	87	67
Pacific Coast	407	241	59
Metro status			
Central	512	273	53
Suburban	1,776	820	46
Independent	593	308	52

[1]The term cities refers also to towns, villages, boroughs, and townships.

[2]Geographic divisions: *New England:* the states of Connecticut, Maine, Massachusetts, New Hampshire, Rhode Island, and Vermont; *Mid-Atlantic:* the states of New Jersey, New York, and Pennsylvania; *East North-Central:* the states of Illinois, Indiana, Michigan, Ohio, and Wisconsin; *West North-Central:* the states of Iowa, Kansas, Minnesota, Missouri, Nebraska, North Dakota, and South Dakota; *South Atlantic:* the states of Delaware, Florida, Georgia, Maryland, North Carolina, South Carolina, Virginia, West Virginia, and the District of Columbia; *East South-Central:* the states of Alabama, Kentucky, Mississippi, and Tennessee; *West South-Central:* the states of Arkansas, Louisiana, Oklahoma, and Texas; *Mountain:* the states of Arizona, Colorado, Idaho, Montana, Nevada, New Mexico, Utah, and Wyoming; *Pacific Coast:* the states of Alaska, California, Hawaii, Oregon, and Washington.

Table 2 Contracts with Public Employee Unions or Associations

Classification	No. reporting (A)	Yes		No	
		No.	% of (A)	No.	% of (A)
Total, all cities	1,019	916	89.9	103	10.1
Population group					
Over 1,000,000	4	4	100.0	0	0.0
500,000–1,000,000	5	5	100.0	0	0.0
250,000–499,999	19	14	73.7	5	26.3
100,000–249,999	74	61	82.4	13	17.6
50,000–99,999	156	142	91.0	14	9.0
25,000–49,999	252	231	91.7	21	8.3
10,000–24,999	509	459	90.2	50	9.8
Geographic division					
New England	97	97	100.0	0	0.0
Mid-Atlantic	142	139	97.9	3	2.1
East North-Central	237	234	98.7	3	1.3
West North-Central	95	79	83.2	16	16.8
South Atlantic	103	80	77.7	23	22.3
East South-Central	17	7	41.2	10	58.8
West South-Central	68	38	55.9	30	44.1
Mountain	48	33	68.8	15	31.3
Pacific Coast	212	209	98.6	3	1.4

METHODOLOGY

In the summer of 1999, ICMA mailed a survey on labor-management relations to all 2,881 U.S. cities with a population of 10,000 or greater. Those cities not responding to the first survey received a second questionnaire. Responses were received from nearly half of those surveyed (Table 1 on page 1).

COLLECTIVE BARGAINING IN THE PUBLIC SECTOR

Three-fourths of responding jurisdictions report having employees who are organized into unions or associations (not shown on the table). Of those, 1,019 provided information about contracts. Almost 90% (916 cities) reported that the local government has entered into contracts with union employees (Table 2).

Of those 916 cities reporting contracts, 888 answered the question about collective bargaining. Collective bargaining is reported by 94% of these jurisdictions (Table 3). All responding cities with populations 500,000 and above and all cities reporting in the New England and Mid-Atlantic geographic divisions participate in collective bargaining.

CHIEF NEGOTIATOR

Negotiations can be lengthy and complex. Cities take different approaches in their organization of the negotiation function. The role of chief negotiator can be filled by any one of several local government positions although it will typically be filled by a high-level position that carries a commensurate level of authority. As the survey results show, population size of the local government seems to influence which position carries responsibility for serving as the chief negotiator (Table 4).

The four largest cities reporting (over 1,000,000 in population) are evenly split between using a full-time labor relations professional or an attorney retained by the city to function as chief negotiator. The majority of cities with a population from 250,000 to 499,999 and from 500,000 to 1,000,000 fill the chief negotiator role with a full-time labor relations professional; approximately 30% of cities in these groups report that the personnel director is the chief negotiator.

For those jurisdictions with a population under 250,000, the percentage that use a full-time labor relations professional drops noticeably, and the percentage that use the city manager or chief administrative officer (CAO) as the chief negotiator increases. Consistently the budget director is least used by jurisdictions that have provided information about the chief negotiator; the department heads, mayors, and consultants are used only a little more often.

Larger cities typically have more funds available to hire a full-time labor-relations professional to serve as chief negotiator. Because large cities have more employees than smaller cities have, negotiations may be more challenging and time-consuming—two factors that warrant a full-time staff person dedicated to union negotiations. People in other positions who serve as chief negotiator have demanding responsibilities in addition to labor negotiations.

A few interesting observations can be made on the basis of responses arrayed by geographic division. Although the overall percentage of cities reporting the mayor as chief negotiator is 4.9%, among cities reporting in the East South-Central geographic division, the percentage is 25. The East South-Central geographic division also shows the highest percentage (66.7%) reporting that the manager or CAO serves as the chief negotiator. Almost 40% of jurisdictions reporting in the Pacific Coast division indicate that the personnel director is the chief negotiator—a percentage that is highest among all geographic divisions and highest among the various positions reported as chief negotiator within cities in the Pacific Coast geographic division. Cities in the Mountain division show the highest percentage (17.9) with a full-time labor relations professional serving as chief negotiator, and the New England and East North-Central jurisdictions show the highest percentages using an attorney in this role.

COLLECTIVE BARGAINING TEAMS

Of the cities answering the questions about whether teams are used in collective bargaining, all 27 cities with a population 250,000 and above indicated that they use a team (not shown). The use of a collective bargaining team diminishes among cities with smaller populations, but in all categories of cities at least 82% report team bargaining. The East South-Central and West South Central divisions show significantly smaller percentages of team bargaining—38.5% and 63.2%, respectively. Even though 63.2% is the majority, it is 23 percentage points below average (86.3%).

Of the 859 cities that indicated use of a team for collective bargaining, 853 provided information about the composition of the team (Table 5). Overall, the majority of cities report a full-time labor-relations professional (60.1%) and an attorney (55.0%) on the team. The next highest percentage of cities report that council members (43.4%) and consultants (43.5%) are on the team.

Data suggest that perhaps the position that was identified as chief negotiator is not included when the team members are reported. For example, of the four cities reporting with a population over 1,000,000, two reported a full-time labor-relations professional as the chief negotiator, and two reported an attorney. When these four cities were asked to identify members of the team, not one identified a full-time labor relations professional as on the team and only one identified an attorney as on the team. There are many of these examples, suggesting that there may be inconsistency in the way jurisdictions report team members. Nonetheless, the responses provide a good snapshot.

Of particular interest is the emergence of positions such as full-time labor-relations professionals and attorneys; holders of these positions are less frequently identified as chief negotiators but are frequently reported on the team. The full-time labor-relations professional is reported as a team member by higher percentages of smaller cities. In fact, the percentage of cities reporting this position on the negotiating team shows an overall increase as population size decreases. This pattern is generally true for the position of city attorney although it is not as

Table 3 Collective Bargaining with Public Employee Unions or Associations

Classification	No. reporting (A)	Yes	
		No.	% of (A)
Total, all cities	888	833	93.8
Population group			
Over 1,000,000	3	3	100.0
500,000–1,000,000	5	5	100.0
250,000–499,999	15	12	80.0
100,000–249,999	63	53	84.1
50,000–99,999	137	129	94.2
25,000–49,999	224	214	95.5
10,000–24,999	441	417	94.6
Geographic division			
New England	91	91	100.0
Mid-Atlantic	127	127	100.0
East North-Central	216	215	99.5
West North-Central	75	69	92.0
South Atlantic	87	70	80.5
East South-Central	10	5	50.0
West South-Central	52	36	69.2
Mountain	39	31	79.5
Pacific Coast	191	189	99.0

clear-cut. The manager is reported as a team member by the majority of all cities with a population over 250,000, but the percentage declines among smaller cities. The assistant manager is reported on the team by higher percentages of cities of all populations than is the manager, with the exception of cities from 250,000 to 499,999 in population. Council members are not reported as team members by any cities with a population of 250,000 and higher, but the percentage of cities reporting the mayor as a member increases as population size decreases. This is also true for the budget director position.

There appear to be some geographic patterns in the composition of the bargaining team although attribution of reason is difficult (not shown). Attorneys are reported on the teams by higher percentages of cities in the central, southern, and western parts of the country. Consultants are reported in higher percentages by the New England, Mid-Atlantic, South Atlantic, and East North-Central cities. Population size may be a factor in these parts of the country as well.

DEADLINE FOR COLLECTIVE BARGAINING

The vast majority of cities (91.0%) do not operate under a legal deadline for conclusion of the collective bargaining process prior to budget submission (not shown). Three of the four cities reporting with a population over 1,000,000 indicate that they are required to conclude the bargaining before the budget is submitted. It may be that in large cities the effect of negotiations related to expenditures such as salaries and wages or insurance benefits would have such a significant impact on the budget that it would be imprudent to submit a budget with unresolved issues.

Although the percentage of cities that do not have a legal deadline is relatively small across the board, not one of the cities in the East South-Central geographic division reports a deadline. Otherwise, there are no pronounced patterns related to a legal deadline for the conclusion of collective bargaining.

STRIKE CONTINGENCY PLANS

Strike contingency plans are designed to provide vital services in the event of a work stoppage. For example, if sanitation

Table 4 Chief Negotiator

Classification	No. reporting (A)	Mayor % of (A)	Manager/ CAO % of (A)	Personnel director % of (A)	Budget director % of (A)	Full-time labor-relations profes-sional % of (A)	Attorney (retained by city) % of (A)	Dept head % of (A)	Consultant % of (A)	Other % of (A)
Total, all cities	978	4.9	32.3	24.4	1.2	6.2	16.1	1.8	4.4	8.6
Population group										
Over 1,000,000	4	0.0	0.0	0.0	0.0	50.0	50.0	0.0	0.0	0.0
500,000-1,000,000	7	0.0	0.0	28.6	0.0	57.1	0.0	0.0	0.0	14.3
250,000-499,999	16	0.0	0.0	31.3	0.0	56.3	6.3	0.0	0.0	6.3
100,000-249,999	69	2.9	13.0	29.0	1.4	26.1	15.9	1.4	4.3	5.8
50,000-99,999	149	2.7	14.8	41.6	1.3	6.7	16.8	1.3	4.0	10.7
25,000-49,999	238	2.9	25.2	32.8	0.8	3.4	15.1	2.9	5.5	11.3
10,000-24,999	495	7.1	45.5	14.5	1.4	2.0	16.6	1.6	4.2	7.1
Geographic division										
New England	99	6.1	45.5	10.1	1.0	4.0	23.2	0.0	2.0	8.1
Mid-Atlantic	145	4.1	54.5	10.3	1.4	2.1	17.2	2.1	0.7	7.6
East North-Central	240	7.9	24.2	24.6	1.3	7.1	22.9	1.3	2.5	8.3
West North-Central	91	2.2	39.6	28.6	0.0	2.2	11.0	0.0	6.6	9.9
South Atlantic	89	3.4	21.3	30.3	2.2	11.2	19.1	3.4	2.2	6.7
East South-Central	12	25.0	66.7	0.0	0.0	0.0	0.0	0.0	0.0	8.3
West South-Central	49	8.2	34.7	22.4	0.0	2.0	12.2	2.0	10.2	8.2
Mountain	39	10.3	28.2	15.4	2.6	17.9	7.7	0.0	7.7	10.3
Pacific Coast	214	0.5	20.1	39.7	1.4	7.9	8.4	3.7	8.4	9.8

workers do not collect solid waste for several days, health and environmental hazards will result. If local government officials are concerned that work stoppages might occur, a contingency plan provides some protection.

Slightly under one-third of the 972 cities reporting indicate that they have a strike contingency plan (Table 6). Population size seems to be a factor; the percentage reporting a contingency plan decreases as population size decreases. The percentage of cities in the East South-Central division is an anomaly. Although only 14 cities in that division responded to the question, 57.1% report a contingency plan. This percentage is at least 17 percentage points higher than that of any other geographic division.

MANAGEMENT RIGHTS CLAUSE IN CONTRACT

A management rights clause preserves the authority of management to manage day-to-day operations. This clause gives management the flexibility necessary to respond to daily concerns and unforeseen crises without having to negotiate each action. Overall, slightly more than 91% of cities report a management rights clause in at least one contract (not shown). (The question asked whether there was a clause in "any contracts.")

Among the population groups, the lowest percentage reporting a management clause is 87.5% of the cities with a population from 250,000 to 499,999 (not shown). But among the geographic divisions, there is more variation. One of the reasons why the cities in the East South-Central division may have a higher incidence of contingency plans is because they have the lowest incidence (60.0% reporting) of management rights clauses in their contracts (not shown). Cities in the West South-Central and Mountain divisions also have lower percentages

reporting a management rights clause (68.5% and 74.4%, respectively).

SPECIFIC MANAGEMENT RIGHTS

Survey respondents were provided with a list of nine specific management rights and asked to identify which, if any, are included in a contract. For virtually every management right listed on the survey instrument, close to 75% or more of respondents reported that the city contract included that management right (Table 7). The one exception is the right to decide whether to contract for services (54.9% reported including that right). This is often one of the most contentious issues in negotiations. (ICMA's survey on alternative service delivery in local government includes questions about employee resistance to contracting out for services and whether the local governments allow their employees to compete in the bid process. For more information see Elaine Morley, "Local Government Use of Alter-

Table 5 Members of Collective Bargaining Team

Classification	No. reporting (A)	Mayor % of (A)	Mgr/ CAO % of (A)	Asst manager % of (A)	Council mbrs % of (A)	Pers director % of (A)	Budget director % of (A)	Atty (retained by city) % of (A)	Dept head % of (A)	Consul- tant % of (A)	Full- time labor relations prof. % of (A)	Other % of (A)
Total, all cities	853	8.0	12.7	30.4	43.4	23.1	10.1	55.0	25.0	43.5	60.1	7.9
Population group												
Over 1,000,000	4	0.0	75.0	75.0	0.0	25.0	0.0	25.0	25.0	50.0	0.0	0.0
500,000-1,000,000	7	0.0	57.1	85.7	0.0	14.3	0.0	42.9	42.9	14.3	14.3	0.0
250,000-499,999	15	6.7	73.3	60.0	0.0	6.7	0.0	40.0	26.7	20.0	26.7	6.7
100,000-249,999	61	4.9	39.3	54.1	13.1	27.9	1.6	67.2	23.0	37.7	49.2	4.9
50,000-99,999	136	3.7	17.6	39.0	26.5	21.3	2.2	80.1	25.7	41.9	62.5	5.9
25,000-49,999	219	4.6	7.8	30.1	36.1	28.8	5.9	68.9	26.5	44.3	63.5	8.2
10,000-24,999	411	11.9	6.1	21.7	60.1	20.7	16.8	38.4	23.8	45.7	61.8	9.0

native Service Delivery Approaches," *Municipal Year Book 1999* [Washington, D.C.: ICMA, 1999], table 5/9.)

Among the various sizes of cities there are some interesting deviations from the overall percentages. Cities with populations from 500,000 to 1,000,000 show the lowest percentages reporting several rights. This is true for setting standards for service, determining employment and promotion standards and procedures, taking disciplinary action, relieving employees from duty with cause, and establishing shifts as necessary. For the latter, although the overall percentage reporting the right to establish shifts is 74.5%, only 28.6% of the cities with a population from 500,000 to 1,000,000 report this right.

Even though a comparatively small percentage of cities in the East South-Central division reported management rights clauses, those that provided information about the content show strong management rights. Of the five reporting cities, 100% report the right to set standards/levels of service; to take disciplinary action; to determine the content of job classifications; to determine missions, policies, budgets, and general operations; and to determine the size and composition of the workforce.

The jurisdictions in the New England and Mid-Atlantic divisions have slightly lower-than-average percentages reporting rights of each type. Although many residents in communities might assume that these rights are typically the purview of management, when labor-management relations are circumscribed by a contract, management's ability to act may be constrained.

TYPES OF EMPLOYEE GRIEVANCES

The types of grievances filed in cities seem to relate in subject matter to some of the areas of decision making protected by management rights clauses. For example, when asked for the top three grievances most often filed in the community, the highest percentage of cities providing information on specific grievance filings

Table 6 Contingency Plans

Classification	No. reporting (A)	Yes No.	Yes % of (A)
Total, all cities	972	300	30.9
Population group			
Over 1,000,000	2	2	100.0
500,000-1,000,000	6	5	83.3
250,000-499,999	19	8	42.1
100,000-249,999	67	28	41.8
50,000-99,999	149	50	33.6
25,000-49,999	240	70	29.2
10,000-24,999	489	137	28.0
Geographic division			
New England	85	10	11.8
Mid-Atlantic	142	47	33.1
East North-Central	234	93	39.7
West North-Central	91	29	31.9
South Atlantic	93	15	16.1
East South-Central	14	8	57.1
West South-Central	64	10	15.6
Mountain	47	11	23.4
Pacific Coast	202	77	38.1

Table 7   Management Rights Specified in Contracts

Classification	No. reporting (A)	To set standard/level of service % of (A)	To determine employment and promotion procedures and standards % of (A)	To take disciplinary action % of (A)	To relieve employees from duty with cause % of (A)	To establish shifts as necessary % of (A)	To determine job classifications % of (A)	To decide whether to contract for services % of (A)	To determine missions, policies, budget, and general operations % of (A)	To determine size and composition of workforce % of (A)	Other % of (A)
Total, all cities	829	84.6	77.1	84.2	78.9	74.5	74.1	54.9	86.9	85.0	6.4
Population group											
Over 1,000,000	4	100.0	75.0	100.0	100.0	75.0	75.0	50.0	100.0	100.0	25.0
500,000-1,000,000	7	57.1	85.7	71.4	71.4	28.6	71.4	42.9	85.7	71.4	14.3
250,000-499,999	13	84.6	76.9	92.3	92.3	69.2	53.8	38.5	76.9	69.2	15.4
100,000-249,999	55	85.5	74.5	80.0	78.2	69.1	70.9	67.3	87.3	85.5	5.5
50,000-99,999	126	89.7	77.8	86.5	76.2	69.0	81.0	56.3	91.3	87.3	8.7
25,000-49,999	214	85.5	75.2	80.4	77.1	77.1	72.4	53.7	84.1	85.0	7.0
10,000-24,999	410	82.7	78.0	85.9	80.2	76.6	73.9	54.1	87.1	84.9	4.9
Geographic division											
New England	88	71.6	68.2	78.4	75.0	67.0	54.5	42.0	86.4	73.9	2.3
Mid-Atlantic	132	71.2	72.0	85.6	75.8	65.9	62.9	44.7	79.5	81.1	3.8
East North-Central	217	87.1	77.0	82.9	78.3	77.9	72.4	59.4	84.8	85.3	6.0
West North-Central	72	91.7	83.3	90.3	83.3	88.9	81.9	65.3	93.1	93.1	8.3
South Atlantic	75	92.0	84.0	89.3	82.7	78.7	90.7	74.7	86.7	89.3	6.7
East South-Central	5	100.0	80.0	100.0	80.0	80.0	100.0	40.0	100.0	100.0	0.0
West South-Central	34	82.4	70.6	91.2	79.4	79.4	79.4	32.4	94.1	85.3	5.9
Mountain	30	90.0	80.0	83.3	76.7	76.7	86.7	56.7	93.3	90.0	13.3
Pacific Coast	176	90.9	80.7	81.3	80.7	71.6	80.1	55.1	89.8	86.9	9.1

report failure to abide by contract (71.5%), termination (33.1%), and performance evaluation (21.1%). (Almost 34% reported "other.") (See Table 8.)

Patterns in the types of grievances filed do not emerge among the population groups, but the geographic divisions show some highs and lows worth noting. The New England (93.7%), East North-Central (85.5%), and the Mid-Atlantic (85.0%) cities show the highest percentages reporting filings for failure to abide by contract. In contrast, cities in the East South-Central division have the lowest percentage reporting this particular grievance. The highest percentage of cities reporting performance evaluation grievances are in the South Atlantic (33.0%) and East South-Central (31.3%) divisions. The East South-Central division also has the highest percentage of cities reporting discrimination grievances (31.3%) and

the lowest percentage reporting failure to abide by the contract (18.8%).

A generally higher percentage of cities in the western half of the country report grievances filed due to terminations than do those in the eastern half.

SUMMARY

Clearly the size of population of a city will influence the organization and management of the labor-relations function. Large cities have more employees and often deliver more services than smaller cities do. Patterns in the data show that large cities tend to dedicate a full-time position to serve as chief negotiator and always use a negotiating team as well. Large cities are more likely to have a deadline for collective bargaining that is related to the budget process and are more likely than small cities to have a strike contingency plan.

Responses from cities in the East South-Central division often differ from the general pattern among cities in other geographic divisions. They have the highest percentage reporting contingency plans and the lowest percentage reporting a management rights clause.

Labor-management relations will always show stellar examples of improvements in service delivery and efficiency when the two groups put their talent and energy together; there will also be times when their needs seem incompatible and relations are strained. Cities that have negotiation expertise and specially allocated full- or part-time staff who keep abreast of the issues and potential problem areas will be in a good position to ensure the smooth functioning of their cities. Many grievances can be avoided through familiarity with contracts, sound management practices, and competent

Table 8   Types of Grievances Filed

Classification	No. reporting (A)	Reduction in workforce % of (A)	Disability % of (A)	Retirement % of (A)	Performance evaluation % of (A)	Discrimination (racial, sexual, etc.) % of (A)	Suitability of position % of (A)	Failure to abide by contract % of (A)	Denial of pay increase % of (A)	Termination % of (A)	Health and safety % of (A)	Other % of (A)
Total, all cities	975	2.7	3.4	1.9	21.1	9.6	13.4	71.5	10.1	33.1	11.3	33.7
Population group												
Over 1,000,000	4	0.0	0.0	0.0	25.0	0.0	25.0	75.0	0.0	25.0	0.0	100.0
500,000-1,000,000	7	0.0	0.0	0.0	14.3	14.3	14.3	85.7	42.9	71.4	0.0	42.9
250,000-499,999	18	0.0	0.0	0.0	16.7	27.8	11.1	44.4	5.6	50.0	5.6	61.1
100,000-249,999	69	1.4	1.4	0.0	24.6	10.1	4.3	72.5	4.3	44.9	5.8	52.2
50,000-99,999	150	0.7	4.0	0.7	18.0	15.3	14.0	71.3	10.0	40.7	11.3	35.3
25,000-49,999	243	2.5	2.9	1.6	20.2	9.1	14.4	74.5	8.2	34.2	8.6	36.2
10,000-24,999	484	3.7	3.9	2.9	22.3	7.4	14.0	70.7	11.6	27.5	13.8	27.7
Geographic division												
New England	95	3.2	5.3	1.1	11.6	1.1	11.6	93.7	10.5	28.4	18.9	28.4
Mid-Atlantic	140	2.1	4.3	7.1	6.4	5.7	20.7	85.0	5.7	20.0	17.9	32.1
East North-Central	228	3.5	3.1	1.8	14.5	4.8	14.9	85.5	8.3	21.1	12.3	32.0
West North-Central	91	2.2	2.2	0.0	29.7	7.7	13.2	62.6	13.2	33.0	18.7	36.3
South Atlantic	94	0.0	1.1	0.0	33.0	14.9	11.7	57.4	14.9	50.0	4.3	36.2
East South-Central	16	6.3	0.0	6.3	31.3	31.3	18.8	18.8	6.3	37.5	12.5	50.0
West South-Central	61	1.6	1.6	1.6	27.9	9.8	11.5	45.9	13.1	42.6	4.9	37.7
Mountain	45	4.4	0.0	2.2	26.7	15.6	13.3	48.9	11.1	48.9	4.4	44.4
Pacific Coast	205	2.9	5.4	0.5	29.8	17.1	8.8	63.4	10.2	43.4	5.4	32.2

supervision. When employees are informed about issues and challenges facing local governments, they may be not only able to propose solutions but also able to tolerate disappointment. An ongoing information-sharing process puts everyone in a better position at the bargaining table.

Table 9 shows responses of individual jurisdictions to questions about contingency plans and management rights.

City of Mt. Pleasant, Michigan – AFSCME Local 1606
Management Rights
Section 11.1. Rights

Except as specifically amended or abridged by the terms of this Agreement, the management and control of the Employer in all of its operations and activities, the determination of all matters of Employer and management policy, operation and location; the location where work will be performed; the direction of the working force, including only by way of illustration and not by way of limitation, the right to hire, discipline, suspend or discharge for just cause, promote, demote, assign, transfer or layoff and recall employees, or to reduce or increase the size of the working force; to establish job classifications of work and the number of employees required and the number of hours in employee work schedules; to establish work schedules and to provide and assign relief personnel; to eliminate totally or partially or combine or otherwise revise existing job classifications; to establish new job classifications; to establish and change form time to time reasonable rules and regulations, including safety rules and regulations; to maintain safety, order and efficiency; to establish job descriptions as deemed desirable and satisfactory work standards; to determine the nature and number of departments to be operated; to discontinue totally or partially or combine or reorganize any part or all of the Employer's operations; is within the sole prerogatives of the Employer. The Employer shall be the exclusive judge of all matters pertaining to the services to be furnished and the methods, procedures, means, equipment and machines required to provide such services; the standards of efficiency and productivity; and the methods, processes, means and materials to be used. The Employer shall have the right to continue and maintain its operations as in the past and prior to the execution of this Agreement with the Union but the Employer shall also have the right to study and use improved methods, means, equipment and outside assistance either in or outside of the Employer's City-wide operations, including subcontracting. It is understood and the Union agrees that the Employer reserves and retains solely and exclusively all of its inherent and customary rights to manage and administer the Employer's operations in all respects. It is provided, however, that these management rights shall not be exercised in violation of any specific provisions of this Bargeement.

Table 9   Responses about Contingency Plans and Management Rights, by Individual Jurisdiction

State and Jurisdiction	1990 pop.	Type	Contingency plan that covers vital services in the event of a work stoppage	Legal deadline for conclusion of collective bargaining prior to budget submission	Management rights clause in any contracts	Set standards and level of service	Determine procedures and standards of selection for employment and promotion	Take disciplinary action	Relieve employees from duty with cause	Establish shifts as necessary	Determine content of job classifications	Decide whether to contract or subcontract for services	Determine missions, policies, budget, and general operations	Determine size and composition of workforce
Alabama														
Dothan	54,143	C	Y											
Homewood	22,922	C	Y	N										
Mountain Brook	19,810	C	Y	N	N									
Northport	17,366	C	N	N	N									
Arkansas														
Benton	18,177	C	Y	N	Y	Y		Y	Y	Y			Y	Y
Little Rock	175,752	C	N	N	Y	Y	Y	Y	Y	Y	Y	Y	Y	Y
Arizona														
Bullhead City	21,951	C	N											
Casa Grande	19,082	C	N	N	N									
Chandler	90,533	C	N	N										
Douglas	13,908	C	N	N	N									
Lake Havasu City	24,363	C	N	N										
Mesa	289,199	C	N	N	N									
Paradise Valley	11,903	T	N	N	N									
Peoria	80,000	C	N	N	Y	Y		Y					Y	
Phoenix	1,159,014	C	Y	Y	Y	Y	Y	Y	Y	Y	Y	Y	Y	Y

State and Jurisdiction	1990 pop.	Type	Contingency plan that covers vital services in the event of a work stoppage	Legal deadline for conclusion of collective bargaining prior to budget submission	Management rights clause in any contracts	Set standards and level of service	Determine procedures and standards of selection for employment and promotion	Take disciplinary action	Relieve employees from duty with cause	Establish shifts as necessary	Determine content of job classifications	Decide whether to contract or subcontract for services	Determine missions, policies, budget, and general operations	Determine size and composition of workforce
Tempe	162,701	C	N											
California														
Alameda	76,459	C	Y	N	Y	Y	Y	Y	Y		Y		Y	
Albany	16,327	C	N	N	N			Y	Y				Y	Y
Anaheim	266,406	C	Y	N	Y	Y	Y	Y	Y	Y	Y	Y	Y	Y
Antioch	76,293	C	Y	N	Y	Y		Y	Y	Y	Y	Y	Y	Y
Arroyo Grande	14,378	C	N	N	Y	Y	Y			Y	Y		Y	Y
Bakersfield	176,264	C	Y	N	Y	Y	Y	Y	Y	Y	Y	Y	Y	Y
Baldwin Park	71,414	C	Y	N	Y	Y	Y	Y	Y	Y	Y	Y	Y	Y
Banning	20,570	C	Y	N	Y	Y	Y	Y	Y	Y	Y	Y	Y	Y
Barstow	21,472	C		N	N									Y
Bell Gardens	42,355	C	N	N	Y	Y	Y			Y	Y	Y	Y	Y
Belmont	24,127	C	Y	N	Y	Y	Y	Y		Y	Y	Y	Y	Y
Benicia	24,437	C	N	N	Y	Y	Y	Y	Y		Y	Y	Y	Y
Berkeley	102,724	C	Y	N	Y	Y	Y	Y	Y		Y		Y	Y
Beverly Hills	31,971	C	Y	N	Y	Y	Y		Y	Y	Y			Y
Brawley	18,923	C	Y	Y	Y	Y	Y	Y	Y	Y	Y	Y	Y	Y
Burbank	93,643	C	Y	N	Y	Y		Y	Y	Y			Y	Y
Burlingame	26,801	C	N	N	Y	Y								Y

State and Jurisdiction	1990 pop.	Type	Contingency plan that covers vital services in the event of a work stoppage	Legal deadline for conclusion of collective bargaining prior to budget submission	Management rights clause in any contracts	Set standards and level of service	Determine procedures and standards of selection for employment and promotion	Take disciplinary action	Relieve employees from duty with cause	Establish shifts as necessary	Determine content of job classifications	Decide whether to contract or subcontract for services	Determine missions, policies, budget, and general operations	Determine size and composition of workforce
Campbell	36,048	C	Y	N	N									
Carson	83,995	C	N	N	Y	Y	Y	Y		Y	Y		Y	Y
Cathedral City	30,085	C	N	N	Y	Y		Y	Y	Y	Y			Y
Ceres	26,314	C	N	N	Y	Y	Y	Y	Y		Y		Y	Y
Cerritos	53,240	C	Y	Y	N									
Chino Hills	37,868	C	N	N	Y									
Chino	59,682	C	N	N	N	Y				Y	Y		Y	Y
Chula Vista	135,000	C	N	N	Y									
Claremont	32,503	C	N	N	Y	Y	Y	Y	Y	Y	Y	Y	Y	Y
Clovis	50,323	C	Y	N	Y	Y	Y	Y	Y	Y	Y	Y	Y	Y
Colton	40,213	C	N	N	N									
Commerce	12,135	C	N	N	Y	Y	Y	Y	Y	Y	Y	Y	Y	Y
Corcoran	13,364	C	N	N	Y	Y	Y	Y	Y	Y	Y	Y	Y	Y
Costa Mesa	96,357	C	N	N	N	Y	Y	Y	Y	Y	Y	Y	Y	Y
Covina	43,207	C	N	N	Y	Y	Y	Y	Y	Y	Y	Y	Y	Y
Cudahy	22,817	C	N	N	Y	Y	Y	Y	Y	Y	Y	Y	Y	Y
Cupertino	40,263	C	Y	N	Y	Y	Y	Y	Y	Y	Y	Y	Y	Y
Cypress	42,655	C	Y	N	Y	Y	Y	Y	Y	Y	Y	Y	Y	Y
Dana Point	31,896	C	N	N	Y	Y	Y	Y	Y	Y	Y	Y	Y	Y
Davis	52,321	C	N	N	Y	Y	Y	Y	Y		Y		Y	
Dinuba	12,743	C	N	N	N									

State and Jurisdiction	1990 pop.	Type	Contingency plan for continuation of vital services in the event of a work stoppage	Legal deadline for conclusion of collective bargaining prior to budget submission	Management rights clause in any contracts	Set standards and level of service	Determine procedures and standards of selection for employment and promotion	Take disciplinary action	Relieve employees from duty with cause	Establish shifts as necessary	Determine content of job classifications	Decide whether to contract or subcontract for services	Determine missions, policies, budget, and general operations	Determine size and composition of workforce
Dixon	10,401	C	N	N	Y	Y	Y	Y		Y	Y		Y	Y
El Cerrito	22,869	C		N	Y	Y	Y	Y	Y		Y	Y	Y	Y
El Monte	106,209	C	N	N	Y	Y	Y	Y	Y		Y	Y	Y	Y
El Segundo	15,223	C		Y	Y	Y	Y	Y		Y	Y		Y	Y
Encinitas	55,386	C	N	N	Y	Y	Y	Y	Y	Y			Y	Y
Escondido	108,635	C	N	N	Y	Y	Y	Y					Y	Y
Eureka	27,025	C	Y	Y	Y	Y	Y	Y	Y				Y	Y
Folsom	29,802	C	Y	N	Y	Y	Y	Y	Y	Y	Y		Y	Y
Foster City	28,176	C	Y	N	Y	Y	Y			Y		Y	Y	Y
Fountain Valley	53,691	C	Y	N	Y	Y	Y	Y	Y	Y	Y	Y	Y	Y
Fresno	396,011	C	Y	Y	Y	Y	Y	Y	Y	Y	Y	Y	Y	Y
Fullerton	122,804	C	N	N	Y	Y	Y	Y	Y	Y	Y	Y	Y	Y
Garden Grove	143,050	C	Y	N	Y	Y	Y	Y	Y	Y	Y	Y	Y	Y
Gardena	51,481	C	Y	N	Y		Y	Y	Y		Y		Y	Y
Glendale	180,038	C	Y	N	Y	Y	Y	Y	Y	Y	Y	Y	Y	Y
Glendora	47,828	C	N	N	Y	Y		Y			Y		Y	Y
Grover Beach	11,656	C	Y	N	Y		Y	Y	Y	Y	Y	Y	Y	Y
Hanford	30,897	C	Y	N	Y	Y	Y	Y	Y	Y	Y		Y	Y
Hemet	43,366	C	Y	N	Y	Y	Y	Y	Y	Y	Y	Y	Y	Y

State and Jurisdiction	1990 pop.	Type	Contingency plan that covers services in the event of a work stoppage	Legal deadline for conclusion of collective bargaining prior to budget submission	Management rights clause in any contracts	Set standards and level of service	Determine procedures and standards of selection for employment and promotion	Take disciplinary action	Relieve employees from duty with cause	Establish shifts as necessary	Determine content of job classifications	Decide whether to contract or subcontract for services	Determine missions, policies, budget, and general operations	Determine size and composition of workforce
Hermosa Beach	18,219	C	Y	N	Y	Y	Y	Y	Y	Y	Y	Y	Y	Y
Hollister	19,212	C	N	N	N									
Huntington Park	56,065	C	N	N										
Indio	36,793	C	N	N	Y									
Inglewood	109,602	C	Y	N	Y	Y	Y	Y	Y	Y	Y	Y	Y	Y
Irvine	110,330	C	Y	N	Y	Y	Y	Y	Y	Y		Y	Y	Y
La Palma	15,392	C	N	N	Y	Y	Y	Y	Y		Y	Y	Y	Y
La Puente	36,955	C	Y	N	Y	Y	Y	Y	Y	Y	Y	Y	Y	Y
Laguna Niguel	44,400	C	N	Y	Y	Y	Y	Y	Y	Y	Y	Y	Y	Y
Lake Elsinore	19,733	C	N	N	Y	Y	Y	Y	Y	Y	Y	Y	Y	Y
Lakewood	73,557	C	Y	N	Y	Y	Y	Y	Y	Y	Y	Y	Y	Y
Larkspur	11,070	C	N	N	Y	Y	Y	Y	Y	Y	Y	Y	Y	Y
Lawndale	27,331	C	N	N	Y		Y	Y	Y	Y				Y
Livermore	56,741	C	N	N	N									
Lodi	54,812	C	Y	N	Y	Y	Y	Y	Y	Y	Y		Y	
Lompoc	37,649	C	Y	N	Y	Y	Y	Y	Y	Y	Y		Y	Y
Los Alamitos	11,676	C	N	N	Y	Y	Y	Y	Y	Y	Y	Y	Y	Y
Los Altos	26,303	C	N	N	Y	Y	Y	Y	Y	Y	Y	Y	Y	Y
Los Banos	14,519	C		N	N									

State and Jurisdiction	1990 pop.	Type	Contingency plan that covers vital services in the event of a work stoppage	Legal deadline for conclusion of collective bargaining prior to budget submission	Management rights clause in any contracts	Set standards and level of service	Determine procedures and standards of selection for employment and promotion	Take disciplinary action	Relieve employees from duty with cause	Establish shifts as necessary	Determine content of job classifications	Decide whether to contract or subcontract for services	Determine missions, policies, budget, and general operations	Determine size and composition of workforce
Los Gatos	27,357	T	Y	N	Y	Y	Y	Y	Y	Y	Y		Y	Y
Madera	29,281	C	Y	N	Y								Y	Y
Manhattan Beach	32,063	C	N	N	Y	Y	Y	Y	Y	Y	Y	Y	Y	Y
Manteca	40,773	C		N	Y	Y	Y			Y	Y		Y	Y
Maywood	27,850	C	N	N	Y	Y	Y	Y	Y	Y	Y		Y	Y
Merced	58,099	C	N	N	Y	Y	Y	Y	Y	Y	Y		Y	Y
Mill Valley	13,038	C	Y	N	N				Y	Y				
Milpitas	50,686	C	N	N	Y	Y	Y	Y	Y		Y		Y	Y
Modesto	182,000	C	N	N	Y	Y	Y	Y	Y					
Montclair	28,434	C	N	N	Y			Y	Y					
Montebello	59,564	C	Y	N	N									
Monterey Park	60,738	C	N	N	Y	Y	Y							
Monterey	31,954	C	N	N	Y									
Moorpark	25,494	C	N	N	Y	Y			Y	Y	Y			
Moraga	15,852	T	Y	N	Y	Y	Y	Y	Y	Y	Y	Y	Y	Y
Moreno Valley	118,779	C	N	N	Y	Y	Y	Y	Y	Y	Y	Y	Y	Y
Murrieta	18,557	C	Y	N	Y	Y	Y	Y	Y	Y	Y	Y	Y	
Napa	61,842	C		N	Y	Y	Y		Y	Y	Y	Y	Y	Y
Newport Beach	66,643	C	N	N	Y	Y	Y	Y	Y	Y	Y	Y	Y	Y

State and Jurisdiction	1990 pop.	Type	Contingency plan that covers vital services in the event of a work stoppage	Legal deadline for conclusion of collective bargaining prior to budget submission	Management rights clause in any contracts	Set standards and level of service	Determine procedures and standards of selection for employment and promotion	Take disciplinary action	Relieve employees from duty with cause	Establish shifts as necessary	Determine content of job classifications	Decide whether to contract or subcontract for services	Determine missions, policies, budget, and general operations	Determine size and composition of workforce
Norco	23,302	C	Y	N	N									Y
Novato	47,585	C	Y	N	Y	Y	Y	Y	Y	Y	Y		Y	Y
Oakland	367,230	C	N	N	Y			Y	Y	Y			Y	
Ontario	133,179	C	N	N	Y	Y	Y	Y	Y	Y	Y	Y	Y	Y
Orinda	16,642	C	N	N	Y	Y	Y	Y	Y		Y	Y	Y	Y
Oxnard	142,216	C	N	N	Y	Y	Y	Y	Y	Y	Y	Y	Y	Y
Pacific Grove	16,117	C	N	N	Y	Y	Y	Y	Y	Y	Y			Y
Pacifica	37,670	C		N	Y	Y	Y	Y	Y	Y	Y		Y	Y
Palm Springs	40,181	C	Y	N	Y	Y				Y		Y		
Palo Alto	55,900	C	N	N	Y	Y	Y	Y	Y	Y	Y	Y	Y	Y
Palos Verdes Estates	13,512	C	Y	N	Y		Y	Y	Y					
Pasadena	131,591	C	N	N	Y	Y	Y	Y	Y	Y	Y	Y	Y	
Petaluma	43,184	C	N	N	N									
Pico Rivera	59,177	C	N	N	Y	Y						Y		Y
Pleasant Hill	31,585	C	Y	N	Y	Y	Y	Y	Y	Y	Y	Y	Y	Y
Pleasanton	52,275	C	N	N	N									
Pomona	134,706	C	N	N	Y			Y	Y					
Porterville	29,563	C	N	N	Y	Y	Y	Y	Y	Y	Y	Y	Y	Y
Rancho Cucamonga	101,409	C	N	N	Y									

State and Jurisdiction	1990 pop.	Type	Contingency plan that covers vital services in the event of a work stoppage	Legal deadline for conclusion of collective bargaining prior to budget submission	Management rights clause in any contracts	Set standards and level of service	Determine procedures and standards of selection for employment and promotion	Take disciplinary action	Relieve employees from duty with cause	Establish shifts as necessary	Determine content of job classifications	Decide whether to contract or subcontract for services	Determine missions, policies, budget, and general operations	Determine size and composition of workforce
Red Bluff	12,363	C	N	N	Y	Y	Y	Y	Y		Y		Y	Y
Redding	66,462	C	N	N	Y	Y	Y	Y		Y	Y		Y	Y
Reedley	15,791	C	N	N	Y	Y	Y	Y	Y	Y	Y		Y	Y
Riverside	226,505	C	Y	N	Y	Y	Y	Y	Y	Y	Y	Y	Y	Y
Rocklin	19,033	C	N	N	Y	Y	Y	Y	Y	Y	Y	Y	Y	Y
Roseville	44,685	C	N	N	Y	Y	Y	Y	Y	Y	Y	Y	Y	Y
Sacramento	388,725	C	Y	N	Y	Y	Y	Y	Y	Y	Y	Y	Y	Y
Salinas	111,757	C	N	N	Y	Y	Y	Y	Y				Y	
San Bernardino	183,474	C	Y	N	Y	Y	Y	Y	Y	Y	Y		Y	Y
San Buenaventura	92,575	C	N	N	Y	Y		Y	Y	Y		Y	Y	Y
San Clemente	41,100	C	N	N	Y							Y		
San Diego	1,171,121	C	Y	Y	Y	Y	Y	Y	Y				Y	Y
San Francisco, City & County	723,959	C	N	N	Y		Y	Y	Y	Y	Y	Y	Y	
San Jose	873,286	C	Y	N			Y	Y	Y		Y		Y	Y
San Juan Capistrano	26,183	C	N	N	N			Y						
San Leandro	68,223	C	N	N	Y	Y	Y	Y	Y	Y	Y		Y	Y
San Luis Obispo	41,958	C	N	N	Y	Y	Y	Y	Y		Y		Y	

State and Jurisdiction	1990 pop.	Type	Contingency plan that covers vital services in the event of a work stoppage	Legal deadline for conclusion of collective bargaining prior to budget submission	Management rights clause in any contracts	Set standards and level of service	Determine procedures and standards of selection for employment and promotion	Take disciplinary action	Relieve employees from duty with cause	Establish shifts as necessary	Determine content of job classifications	Decide whether to contract or subcontract for services	Determine missions, policies, budget, and general operations	Determine size and composition of workforce
San Marino	12,959	C	N	N	Y								Y	
San Pablo	25,158	C	N	N	Y	Y	Y	Y	Y	Y			Y	
Sanger	16,839	C	Y	N	Y	Y	Y	Y	Y	Y	Y		Y	Y
Santa Ana	293,742	C	N	N	Y	Y	Y	Y	Y	Y	Y	Y	Y	Y
Santa Barbara	85,571	C	Y	N	Y	Y	Y	Y				Y	Y	Y
Santa Clara	98,726	C	N	N	Y	Y	Y	Y	Y	Y	Y	Y	Y	Y
Santa Cruz	49,040	C	N	N	Y	Y	Y	Y			Y	Y	Y	Y
Santa Fe Springs	15,520	C	Y	N	Y	Y								
Santa Maria	61,284	C	Y	N	Y	Y	Y	Y	Y	Y	Y	Y	Y	Y
Santa Monica	91,405	C	N	N	Y	Y	Y	Y	Y	Y	Y	Y	Y	Y
Santa Rosa	132,966	C	Y	Y	Y	Y	Y	Y	Y	Y	Y	Y	Y	Y
Santee	52,902	C	N	N	Y	Y	Y	Y	Y	Y	Y		Y	Y
Saratoga	28,061	C	N	N	Y	Y	Y	Y	Y		Y	Y	Y	Y
Selma	14,757	C	N	N	N									
Solana Beach	12,962	C	N	N	Y									
South San Francisco	54,312	C	N	N	Y	Y	Y	Y	Y				Y	
Stockton	210,943	C	Y	N	Y	Y	Y	Y	Y	Y	Y	Y	Y	
Suisun City	22,686	C	Y	N	N									Y
Sunnyvale	117,229	C	N	N	Y								Y	Y

State and Jurisdiction	1990 pop.	Type	Contingency plan that covers vital services in the event of a work stoppage	Legal deadline for conclusion of collective bargaining prior to budget submission	Management rights clause in any contracts	Set standards and level of service	Determine procedures and standards of selection for employment and promotion	Take disciplinary action	Relieve employees from duty with cause	Establish shifts as necessary	Determine content of job classifications	Decide whether to contract or subcontract for services	Determine missions, policies, budget, and general operations	Determine size and composition of workforce
Susanville	12,130	C	Y	N	N									
Temecula	35,000	C	Y	N	Y	Y	Y	Y	Y	Y	Y	Y	Y	Y
Thousand Oaks	104,352	C	N	N	N									
Torrance	133,107	C	Y	N	Y									
Ukiah	14,599	C		N	Y								Y	Y
Union City	53,762	C												
Upland	63,374	C		N	Y	Y					Y		Y	Y
Vallejo	109,199	C	Y	Y	Y	Y	Y	Y	Y		Y			Y
Vista	71,872	C	N	N	Y	Y	Y	Y	Y		Y		Y	Y
Wasco	12,412	C	N	N	Y	Y	Y	Y	Y	Y	Y	Y	Y	Y
West Sacramento	28,898	C	N	N	Y	Y				Y			Y	Y
Westminster	78,118	C	Y	N	Y	Y	Y	Y	Y	Y	Y		Y	Y
Whittier	77,671	C	N	N	Y	Y	Y	Y	Y	Y	Y	Y	Y	Y
Windsor	12,002	T	N	N	Y	Y	Y	Y	Y	Y	Y	Y	Y	Y
Yorba Linda	52,422	C	N	N	Y	Y	Y	Y	Y	Y	Y	Y	Y	Y
Colorado														
Boulder	85,127	C	N	Y	Y	Y	Y	Y	Y	Y	Y	Y	Y	Y
Canon City	12,687	C	N	N	N									
Colorado Springs	344,400	C	N											

State and Jurisdiction	1990 pop.	Type	Contingency plan that covers vital services in the event of a work stoppage	Legal deadline for conclusion of collective bargaining prior to budget submission	Management rights clause in any contracts	Set standards and level of service	Determine procedures and standards of selection for employment and promotion	Take disciplinary action	Relieve employees from duty with cause	Establish shifts as necessary	Determine content of job classifications	Decide whether to contract or subcontract for services	Determine missions, policies, budget, and general operations	Determine size and composition of workforce
Commerce City	16,466	C	N	N										
Englewood	29,387	C	N	Y	Y	Y	Y	Y	Y	Y	Y	Y	Y	Y
Fountain	10,754	C		N	N									
Grand Junction	32,893	C	N											
Greeley	60,536	C	N	N	Y	Y	Y	Y	Y	Y	Y	Y	Y	Y
Littleton	33,685	C	Y	N	Y	Y	Y	Y	Y	Y	Y	Y	Y	Y
Pueblo	98,640	C	N	Y	Y	Y	Y	Y			Y	Y	Y	Y
Connecticut														
Ansonia	18,403	C	N	Y	Y	Y	Y	Y	Y	Y			Y	Y
Avon	13,937	T	N	Y	Y	Y	Y	Y	Y	Y	Y	Y	Y	Y
Bristol	60,640	C		N	Y								Y	Y
Cheshire	25,684	T	N	N	Y	Y	Y	Y	Y	Y	Y		Y	Y
Coventry	10,063	T	N	N	Y	Y		Y	Y					Y
Darien	18,196	T	N	N	Y	Y	Y	Y	Y		Y		Y	
East Hampton	10,428	T	N	N	Y									
East Haven	26,144	T	N	N	Y			Y	Y	Y				Y
East Lyme	15,340	T		N	Y									
Hartford	139,739	C	Y	N	Y	Y	Y	Y	Y	Y	Y	Y	Y	Y
Ledyard	14,913	T	N	N	Y			Y						
Manchester	51,618	T	N	N	Y	Y	Y	Y			Y		Y	

State and Jurisdiction	1990 pop.	Type	Contingency plan that covers vital services in the event of a work stoppage	Legal deadline for conclusion of collective bargaining prior to budget submission	Management rights clause in any contracts	Set standards and level of service	Determine procedures and standards of selection for employment and promotion	Take disciplinary action	Relieve employees from duty with cause	Establish shifts as necessary	Determine content of job classifications	Decide whether to contract or subcontract for services	Determine missions, policies, budget, and general operations	Determine size and composition of workforce
New Haven	130,474	C		N	Y		Y	Y		Y			Y	Y
Newington	29,208	T	N	N	Y	Y		Y				Y	Y	Y
Newtown	20,779	T	N	N	Y	Y	Y	Y	Y	Y	Y		Y	Y
North Haven	22,247	T	N	N	Y								Y	Y
Norwich	37,391	C	N	N	Y	Y	Y	Y	Y	Y	Y	Y	Y	Y
Orange	12,830	T	N	N	Y	Y	Y	Y	Y	Y	Y		Y	Y
Plainville	17,392	T	N	N	Y	Y	Y	Y			Y		Y	Y
Rocky Hill	16,554	T	N		Y	Y		Y						
Shelton	35,418	C	N	N	Y	Y	Y	Y	Y	Y	Y	Y	Y	Y
Southington	38,518	T	N	N	Y	Y	Y	Y	Y	Y	Y	Y	Y	Y
Stafford	11,091	T	N	N	Y	Y	Y	Y	Y	Y	Y	Y	Y	Y
Stratford	49,389	T	N	N	Y	Y	Y	Y	Y			Y	Y	Y
Trumbull	32,016	T	N	N	Y	Y								
Vernon	29,841	T	N	N	Y	Y		Y	Y	Y	Y	Y	Y	Y
West Hartford	60,110	T	N	N	Y			Y	Y	Y	Y	Y	Y	Y
Wethersfield	25,651	T	N	N	Y	Y	Y	Y	Y	Y	Y	Y	Y	Y
Windsor	27,817	T	N	N	Y	Y	Y	Y	Y	Y	Y	Y	Y	Y
Delaware														
Newark	25,098	C	N	N	Y	Y	Y	Y	Y		Y	Y	Y	Y
Wilmington	71,529	C	N	N	Y	Y	Y	Y	Y	Y	Y	Y	Y	Y

State and Jurisdiction	1990 pop.	Type	Contingency plan that covers conclusion of vital services in the event of a work stoppage	Legal deadline for conclusion of collective bargaining prior to budget submission	Management rights clause in any contracts	Set standards and level of service	Determine procedures and standards of selection for employment and promotion	Take disciplinary action	Relieve employees from duty with cause	Establish shifts as necessary	Determine content of job classifications	Decide whether to contract or subcontract for services	Determine missions, policies, budget, and general operations	Determine size and composition of workforce
District of Columbia	606,900	6	Y	N	Y	Y	Y	Y	Y	Y	Y	Y	Y	Y
Florida														
Aventura	14,914	C		N	Y	Y	Y	Y	Y	Y	Y	Y	Y	Y
Boca Raton	61,492	C	N	N	Y	Y	Y	Y	Y	Y	Y	Y	Y	Y
Boynton Beach	46,194	C	N	N	Y	Y	Y	Y	Y	Y	Y	Y	Y	Y
Bradenton	43,779	C		N	Y	Y	Y	Y	Y	Y				
Cape Coral	74,991	C	Y	Y	Y	Y	Y	Y	Y		Y	Y	Y	Y
Casselberry	20,736	C	N	N	N									
Coconut Creek	27,485	C	N	N	Y	Y	Y	Y	Y	Y	Y	Y	Y	Y
Cooper City	20,791	C	N	N	Y	Y	Y	Y	Y	Y	Y	Y	Y	Y
Coral Springs	105,275	C	N	N	Y	Y	Y	Y	Y	Y	Y	Y	Y	Y
Davie	47,217	T	N	N	Y			Y	Y		Y	Y	Y	Y
Daytona Beach	61,921	C	N	N	Y	Y	Y	Y	Y	Y	Y	Y	Y	Y
Delray Beach	47,181	C	N	N	Y	Y	Y	Y	Y	Y	Y	Y	Y	Y
Deltona	50,828	C	N	N	Y	Y	Y	Y	Y	Y	Y		Y	Y
Edgewater	15,337	C	N	N	Y	Y	Y	Y	Y	Y	Y	Y	Y	Y
Fort Lauderdale	149,377	C	N	N	Y	Y	Y	Y	Y	Y	Y	Y	Y	Y

State and Jurisdiction	1990 pop.	Type	Contingency plan that covers vital services in the event of a work stoppage	Legal deadline for conclusion of collective bargaining prior to budget submission	Management rights clause in any contracts	Set standards and level of service	Determine procedures and standards of selection for employment and promotion	Take disciplinary action	Relieve employees from duty with cause	Establish shifts as necessary	Determine content of job classifications	Decide whether to contract or subcontract for services	Determine missions, policies, budget, and general operations	Determine size and composition of workforce
Fort Pierce	36,830	C	N	N	Y	Y	Y	Y	Y	Y	Y	Y	Y	Y
Fort Walton Beach	21,471	C	N	N	Y	Y	Y	Y	Y	Y	Y	Y	Y	
Gainesville	84,770	C	Y	N	Y	Y	Y	Y	Y	Y	Y	Y		Y
Greenacres	18,683	C	Y	N	Y	Y		Y		Y	Y	Y	Y	Y
Hollywood	121,697	C	N	N	Y	Y	Y	Y	Y		Y	Y	Y	Y
Jacksonville Beach	17,839	C	N	N	Y	Y	Y	Y	Y	Y	Y	Y	Y	Y
Jacksonville	635,000	C	Y	N	Y		Y	Y	Y	Y	Y	Y	Y	Y
Jupiter	26,753	T	N	N	Y	Y	Y	Y	Y	Y	Y		Y	Y
Key West	25,339	C	N	N	Y	Y	Y	Y		Y	Y		Y	Y
Lake City	10,005	C	N	N	Y	Y	Y	Y	Y	Y	Y	Y	Y	Y
Largo	65,674	C	N	N	Y	Y	Y	Y	Y	Y	Y	Y	Y	Y
Lauderdale Lakes	27,341	C	N	N	Y	Y	Y	Y	Y	Y	Y	Y	Y	Y
Lauderhill	49,708	C		N	Y								Y	
Leesburg	14,903	C	N	N	Y	Y	Y	Y	Y	Y	Y	Y	Y	Y
Lighthouse Point	10,378	C	N	N	Y	Y	Y	Y	Y	Y	Y	Y	Y	Y
Melbourne	59,646	C	N	N	Y									
Miami Springs	13,268	C	N	N	Y	Y				Y	Y		Y	
Miramar	40,663	C	N	N	Y	Y	Y	Y	Y	Y	Y	Y	Y	Y

State and Jurisdiction	1990 pop.	Type	Contingency plan for services in the event of a work stoppage	Legal deadline for conclusion of collective bargaining prior to budget submission	Management rights clause in any contracts	Set standards and level of service	Determine procedures and standards of selection for employment and promotion	Take disciplinary action	Relieve employees from duty with cause	Establish shifts as necessary	Determine content of job classifications	Decide whether to contract or subcontract for services	Determine missions, policies, budget, and general operations	Determine size and composition of workforce
New Port Richey	14,044	C	N	N	Y	Y	Y	Y	Y	Y	Y	Y	Y	Y
Niceville	10,507	C	N	N	Y	Y	Y	Y	Y	Y	Y		Y	Y
North Lauderdale	26,506	C	N	N	Y	Y	Y	Y	Y	Y	Y	Y	Y	Y
North Miami Beach	35,359	C	N	N	Y	Y	Y	Y	Y	Y	Y	Y	Y	Y
Oakland Park	26,326	C	N	N	Y	Y	Y	Y	Y	Y	Y	Y	Y	Y
Ocala	42,045	C	N	N	Y	Y	Y	Y	Y	Y	Y		Y	Y
Ocoee	12,778	C	N	N	N	Y	Y	Y	Y	Y	Y	Y	Y	Y
Orlando	164,693	C	N	N	Y	Y	Y	Y		Y	Y	Y	Y	Y
Ormond Beach	29,721	C	N	N	Y	Y	Y		Y	Y	Y	Y	Y	Y
Palatka	10,201	C	N	N	Y	Y	Y	Y	Y	Y	Y	Y	Y	Y
Palm Bay	62,632	C	N	N	Y	Y	Y	Y	Y	Y	Y	Y	Y	Y
Panama City	34,378	C	N	N	Y	Y	Y	Y	Y	Y	Y	Y	Y	Y
Pembroke Pines	65,452	C	Y	N	Y	Y	Y	Y	Y	Y	Y		Y	Y
Pensacola	58,165	C	N	N	Y	Y								
Pinellas Park	43,426	C	N	N		Y					Y	Y		Y
Pompano Beach	72,411	C	N	N	Y	Y	Y	Y	Y	Y	Y	Y	Y	Y
Port Orange	35,317	C	N	N	Y	Y								Y

State and Jurisdiction	1990 pop.	Type	Contingency plan that covers vital services in the event of a work stoppage	Legal deadline for conclusion of collective bargaining prior to budget submission	Management rights clause in any contracts	Set standards and level of service	Determine procedures and standards of selection for employment and promotion	Take disciplinary action	Relieve employees from duty with cause	Establish shifts as necessary	Determine content of job classifications	Decide whether to contract or subcontract for services	Determine missions, policies, budget, and general operations	Determine size and composition of workforce
Port St. Lucie	55,866	C	Y	N	Y	Y	Y	Y	Y	Y	Y	Y	Y	Y
Punta Gorda	10,747	C	N	N	Y	Y				Y		Y		Y
Riviera Beach	27,639	C	N	N	Y	Y			Y	Y	Y	Y	Y	Y
Rockledge	16,023	C	N	N	Y		Y	Y	Y	Y	Y	Y	Y	Y
Safety Harbor	15,124	C	N	N	Y	Y	Y	Y	Y	Y	Y	Y	Y	Y
Sanford	32,387	C		N	Y	Y	Y	Y	Y	Y	Y	Y	Y	Y
Sarasota	50,961	C	N	N	Y	Y	Y	Y		Y	Y	Y		
Sebastian	10,205	C	N	N	Y	Y	Y	Y	Y		Y		Y	Y
South Daytona	12,482	C	N	N	Y	Y	Y	Y	Y	Y	Y	Y	Y	Y
St. Petersburg	238,629	C	N	N	Y	Y	Y	Y	Y	Y	Y	Y	Y	Y
Stuart	11,936	C	Y	N	Y	Y	Y	Y	Y	Y	Y	Y	Y	Y
Tallahassee	124,773	C	N	N	Y	Y	Y	Y	Y	Y	Y	Y	Y	Y
Tamarac	44,822	C	N	N	Y	Y	Y	Y	Y	Y	Y	Y	Y	Y
Tampa	280,015	C	N	N	Y	Y	Y	Y	Y	Y	Y	Y	Y	Y
Tarpon Springs	17,906	C	N	N	Y									
Temple Terrace	16,444	C	N	N	Y	Y	Y	Y	Y	Y	Y	Y	Y	Y
Venice	16,922	C	Y	N	Y	Y	Y	Y	Y	Y	Y	Y	Y	Y

State and Jurisdiction	1990 pop.	Type	Contingency plan in the event of a work stoppage	Legal deadline for conclusion of collective bargaining prior to budget submission	Management rights clause in any contracts	Set standards and level of service	Determine procedures and standards of selection for employment and promotion	Take disciplinary action	Relieve employees from duty with cause	Establish shifts as necessary	Determine content of job classifications	Decide whether to contract or subcontract for services	Determine missions, policies, budget, and general operations	Determine size and composition of workforce
Vero Beach	17,350	C	N	N	Y	Y	Y	Y	Y	Y	Y	Y		Y
West Palm Beach	67,643	C	N	N	Y	Y	Y	Y	Y	Y	Y	Y	Y	Y
Winter Haven	24,725	C	N	N	Y	Y	Y	Y	Y	Y	Y	Y	Y	Y
Winter Springs	22,151	C	Y	N	Y	Y	Y	Y	Y	Y	Y	Y	Y	Y
Georgia														
Albany	78,122	C												
Savannah	137,560	C	N	N	N									
Hawaii														
Hilo	45,877	C	Y	N	Y									
Idaho														
Boise City	126,685	C		N	Y	Y	Y	Y	Y	Y	Y	Y	Y	Y
Caldwell	18,400	C	N	N	N									
Lewiston	28,082	C	Y	N	Y	Y	Y	Y	Y	Y	Y	Y	Y	Y
Pocatello	46,080	C	N	N										
Twin Falls	27,591	C	N	N	Y	Y	Y	Y	Y	Y	Y	Y	Y	Y
Illinois														
Addison	33,175	V	N	N	Y	Y	Y	Y	Y	Y	Y	Y	Y	Y
Algonquin	11,663	V	N	N	Y	Y	Y	Y	Y	Y	Y		Y	Y
Arlington Heights	75,460	V		N	Y									Y

State and Jurisdiction	1990 pop.	Type	Contingency plan that covers vital services in the event of a work stoppage	Legal deadline for conclusion of collective bargaining prior to budget submission	Management rights clause in any contracts	Set standards and level of service	Determine procedures and standards of selection for employment and promotion	Take disciplinary action	Relieve employees from duty with cause	Establish shifts as necessary	Determine content of job classifications	Decide whether to contract or subcontract for services	Determine missions, policies, budget, and general operations	Determine size and composition of workforce
Batavia	17,076	C	N	N	Y	Y	Y	Y	Y	Y	Y	Y	Y	Y
Bloomington	51,972	C	N	N	Y	Y	Y	Y	Y	Y	Y	Y	Y	Y
Blue Island	21,203	C	Y	N	Y	Y	Y	Y	Y	Y	Y			
Brookfield	18,876	V	N	N	Y	Y	Y	Y	Y	Y	Y	Y	Y	Y
Buffalo Grove	36,427	V	N	N	Y	Y		Y		Y	Y	Y	Y	Y
Carol Stream	31,716	V	Y	N	Y	Y	Y	Y					Y	Y
Carpentersville	23,049	V	Y	N	Y	Y	Y	Y	Y		Y		Y	Y
Cary	10,043	V	Y	N	Y	Y	Y	Y	Y	Y	Y	Y	Y	Y
Champaign	63,502	C	Y	N	Y	Y	Y	Y	Y	Y	Y	Y	Y	Y
Charleston	20,398	C	N	N	Y	Y		Y	Y	Y	Y		Y	
Chicago Ridge	13,643	V	N	N	Y			Y	Y	Y	Y		Y	
Collinsville	22,446	C	N	N	Y	Y	Y	Y	Y	Y	Y		Y	Y
Crest Hill	10,643	C	Y	N	Y	Y	Y	Y	Y	Y	Y	Y	Y	Y
Crystal Lake	24,512	C	Y	N	Y	Y	Y	Y	Y	Y	Y	Y	Y	Y
Darien	20,556	C	N	N	Y	Y	Y	Y	Y	Y	Y	Y	Y	Y
Deerfield	17,327	V	N	N	Y	Y	Y	Y	Y	Y	Y	Y	Y	Y
Des Plaines	53,223	C	Y	N	Y	Y	Y	Y				Y	Y	Y
Dolton	23,930	V	N	N	Y	Y		Y	Y	Y			Y	Y

State and Jurisdiction	1990 pop.	Type	Contingency plan that covers vital services in the event of a work stoppage	Legal deadline for conclusion of collective bargaining prior to budget submission	Management rights clause in any contracts	Set standards and level of service	Determine procedures and standards of selection for employment and promotion	Take disciplinary action	Relieve employees from duty with cause	Establish shifts as necessary	Determine content of job classifications	Decide whether to contract or subcontract for services	Determine missions, policies, budget, and general operations	Determine size and composition of workforce
Downers Grove	46,858	V	N	N	Y	Y	Y	Y	Y	Y	Y		Y	Y
Elk Grove Village	33,429	V	Y	N	Y	Y	Y	Y	Y	Y	Y	Y	Y	Y
Elmwood Park	23,206	V	N	N	Y	Y	Y	Y		Y	Y	Y		Y
Evergreen Park	20,874	V	Y	N	Y	Y	Y	Y		Y				
Fairview Heights	14,768	C	N	N	Y		Y	Y				Y		
Galesburg	33,530	C	Y	N	Y									
Geneva	12,617	C	Y	Y	Y	Y	Y	Y	Y	Y	Y	Y	Y	Y
Glen Ellyn	24,944	V	N	N	Y									
Glendale Heights	27,973	V	N	N	Y	Y	Y	Y	Y	Y	Y	Y	Y	Y
Godfrey	15,671	V	N	N	Y			Y	Y	Y			Y	Y
Gurnee	13,701	V	N	N	Y	Y	Y	Y	Y	Y	Y	Y	Y	Y
Hoffman Estates	46,561	V	N	N	Y	Y	Y	Y	Y	Y	Y	Y	Y	Y
Jacksonville	19,324	C	N	N	Y	Y	Y	Y		Y	Y	Y	Y	Y
Justice	11,137	V	N	N	Y	Y	Y	Y	Y	Y	Y		Y	Y
Kewanee	12,969	C	N	N	Y	Y	Y	Y	Y		Y	Y	Y	Y
La Grange	15,362	V	N	N	Y	Y	Y	Y	Y	Y	Y	Y	Y	Y
Lake Forest	17,836	C	N	N	Y	Y	Y	Y	Y	Y	Y	Y	Y	Y

State and Jurisdiction	1990 pop.	Type	Contingency plan that covers vital services in the event of a work stoppage	Legal deadline for conclusion of collective bargaining prior to budget submission	Management rights clause in any contracts	Set standards and level of service	Determine procedures and standards of selection for employment and promotion	Take disciplinary action	Relieve employees from duty with cause	Establish shifts as necessary	Determine content of job classifications	Decide whether to contract or subcontract for services	Determine missions, policies, budget, and general operations	Determine size and composition of workforce
Lake Zurich	14,947	V	Y	N	Y	Y	Y	Y	Y	Y	Y	Y	Y	Y
Libertyville	19,174	V	N	N	Y	Y	Y	Y	Y	Y	Y	Y	Y	Y
Lisle	19,512	V	N	N	Y	Y	Y	Y	Y	Y	Y	Y	Y	Y
Lombard	39,408	V	N	N	Y	Y	Y	Y	Y	Y	Y	Y	Y	Y
Matteson	11,378	V	Y	N	Y	Y	Y	Y	Y	Y	Y	Y	Y	Y
Moline	43,202	C	N	N	N								Y	
Morton Grove	22,408	V	Y	N	Y									
Mount Prospect	53,170	V	Y	N	Y	Y	Y	Y	Y	Y	Y	Y	Y	Y
Naperville	118,835	C	Y	N	Y	Y	Y	Y	Y	Y	Y	Y	Y	Y
Normal	40,023	T	N	N	Y	Y	Y	Y	Y	Y	Y		Y	Y
Oak Forest	26,203	C	N	N	Y					Y				
Park Forest	24,656	V	N	N	Y	Y	Y	Y	Y	Y			Y	
Park Ridge	36,175	C	Y	N	Y									
Pekin	32,254	C	N	N	Y	Y								Y
Peoria	113,513	C	N	N	Y	Y	Y	Y	Y	Y	Y	Y	Y	Y
Pontiac	11,428	C	Y	N	Y	Y	Y	Y	Y	Y	Y	Y	Y	Y
Rantoul	17,212	V	Y	N	Y	Y	Y	Y	Y	Y	Y	Y	Y	Y
River Forest	11,669	V	N	N	Y	Y	Y	Y	Y	Y	Y	Y	Y	Y
Riverdale	13,671	V	N	N	Y	Y		Y	Y	Y			Y	Y
Rock Island	40,552	C	Y	N	Y	Y	Y	Y	Y	Y	Y	Y	Y	Y

State and Jurisdiction	1990 pop.	Type	Contingency plan that covers vital services in the event of a work stoppage	Legal deadline for conclusion of collective bargaining prior to budget submission	Management-rights clause in any contracts	Set standards and level of service	Determine procedures and standards of selection for employment and promotion	Take disciplinary action	Relieve employees from duty with cause	Establish shifts as necessary	Determine content of job classifications	Decide whether to contract or subcontract for services	Determine missions, policies, budget, and general operations	Determine size and composition of workforce
Rockford	142,815	C	N	N	Y	Y			Y	Y		Y	Y	Y
Roselle	20,819	V	N	N	Y			Y	Y	Y		Y	Y	Y
Skokie	59,432	V	N	N	Y	Y	Y	Y	Y	Y	Y	Y	Y	Y
St. Charles	22,501	C	N	N	Y	Y	Y		Y	Y	Y		Y	Y
Sterling	15,132	C	N	N	Y	Y	Y	Y	Y	Y	Y	Y	Y	Y
Streamwood	30,987	V	N	N	Y	Y	Y	Y	Y	Y	Y	Y	Y	Y
Streator	14,121	C	Y	N	Y	Y	Y					Y		Y
Tinley Park	37,121	V	N	N	Y									
Villa Park	22,253	V	Y	N	Y	Y	Y	Y	Y	Y	Y	Y	Y	Y
Warrenville	11,333	C	N	N	Y	Y	Y	Y	Y	Y			Y	Y
Westchester	17,301	V	Y	N	Y	Y	Y	Y	Y	Y			Y	Y
Western Springs	11,984	V	N	N	Y	Y	Y	Y	Y	Y			Y	Y
Westmont	21,228	V		N	Y	Y	Y	Y	Y	Y	Y		Y	Y
Wheeling	29,911	V	N	N	Y	Y	Y	Y	Y	Y	Y		Y	Y
Wilmette	26,690	V	Y	N	Y	Y	Y	Y	Y	Y	Y	Y	Y	Y
Wood Dale	12,425	C	N	N	Y	Y	Y	Y	Y	Y	Y		Y	Y
Wood River	11,490	C	Y	N	Y	Y	Y	Y	Y	Y	Y		Y	Y
Woodstock	14,353	C	N	N	Y	Y							Y	
Zion	19,775	C	N	N	Y	Y	Y	Y						

State and Jurisdiction	1990 pop.	Type	Contingency plan that covers vital services in the event of a work stoppage	Legal deadline for conclusion of collective bargaining prior to budget submission	Management rights clause in any contracts	Set standards and level of service	Determine procedures and standards of selection for employment and promotion	Take disciplinary action	Relieve employees from duty with cause	Establish shifts as necessary	Determine content of job classifications	Decide whether to contract or subcontract for services	Determine missions, policies, budget, and general operations	Determine size and composition of workforce
Indiana														
Bloomington	62,015	C	N	Y	Y		Y	Y	Y	Y	Y	Y		
Evansville	126,272	C	Y	N	Y	Y	Y	Y	Y	Y	Y	Y	Y	
Fort Wayne	202,904	C	Y	N	Y	Y	Y		Y		Y		Y	Y
Frankfort	14,754	C												
Gary	116,646	C	N	N	Y	Y		Y	Y					
Highland	23,696	T	N	N	N									
Huntington	16,389	C	N	N	Y	Y	Y	Y	Y	Y			Y	Y
Lake Station	13,899	C	N	Y	N									
Mishawaka	42,608	C	N	N	Y		Y	Y	Y	Y		Y	Y	
Richmond	38,705	C	N	N	Y		Y		Y		Y		Y	
Seymour	15,605	C	N	N	Y									
Terre Haute	57,475	C	N	Y	Y									
Valparaiso	24,414	C	Y	N	Y	Y	Y	Y	Y	Y			Y	Y
Iowa														
Ankeny	18,482	C	N	Y	Y	Y	Y	Y	Y			Y	Y	
Bettendorf	28,132	C	N	Y	Y									
Boone	12,392	C	N	Y	Y									
Burlington	27,208	C	N	Y	Y									
Clinton	29,201	C	N	Y	Y	Y	Y	Y	Y	Y	Y		Y	Y
Coralville	10,347	C	N	N	Y	Y	Y	Y	Y	Y	Y	Y	Y	Y

State and Jurisdiction	1990 pop.	Type	Contingency plan that covers vital services in the event of a work stoppage	Legal deadline for conclusion of collective bargaining prior to budget submission	Management rights clause in any contracts	Set standards and level of service	Determine procedures and standards of selection for employment and promotion	Take disciplinary action	Relieve employees from duty with cause	Establish shifts as necessary	Determine content of job classifications	Decide whether to contract or subcontract for services	Determine missions, policies, budget, and general operations	Determine size and composition of workforce
Council Bluffs	54,315	C	N	Y	Y	Y	Y	Y	Y	Y	Y	Y	Y	Y
Davenport	95,333	C	N	Y	Y			Y				Y	Y	Y
Des Moines	193,187	C	Y	Y	Y	Y	Y	Y	Y	Y			Y	Y
Dubuque	57,546	C	N	Y	Y	Y	Y	Y	Y	Y	Y	Y	Y	Y
Indianola	11,340	C	N	N	Y	Y	Y	Y	Y	Y	Y	Y	Y	Y
Iowa City	59,738	C	N	Y	Y	Y	Y	Y	Y	Y		Y	Y	Y
Keokuk	12,451	C	N	Y	Y	Y	Y	Y	Y	Y	Y			Y
Marion	20,403	C	N	Y	N									
Marshalltown	25,178	C	N	Y	Y	Y	Y	Y	Y	Y	Y		Y	Y
Muscatine	22,881	C	Y	N	Y	Y		Y	Y	Y	Y			Y
Newton	14,789	C	N	N	Y	Y	Y	Y	Y	Y		Y	Y	
Oskaloosa	10,632	C	N	Y	Y	Y	Y	Y	Y	Y		Y	Y	Y
Ottumwa	24,488	C	N	Y	Y									
Sioux City	80,505	C	N	Y	Y	Y	Y	Y	Y	Y	Y	Y	Y	Y
Waterloo	66,467	C	N	N	Y	Y	Y	Y			Y	Y	Y	Y
Kansas														
Arkansas City	12,762	C	N											
Hays	18,632	C	N	N	Y									
Junction City	20,604	C	N	Y	Y	Y	Y	Y	Y	Y	Y		Y	Y

State and Jurisdiction	1990 pop.	Type	Contingency plan that covers vital services in the event of a work stoppage	Legal deadline for conclusion of collective bargaining prior to budget submission	Management rights clause in any contracts	Set standards and level of service	Determine procedures and standards of selection for employment and promotion	Take disciplinary action	Relieve employees from duty with cause	Establish shifts as necessary	Determine content of job classifications	Decide whether to contract or subcontract for services	Determine missions, policies, budget, and general operations	Determine size and composition of workforce
Kansas City	151,521	C	N	N	Y	Y	Y	Y	Y	Y	Y		Y	Y
Lawrence	65,608	C	Y	Y	Y	Y	Y	Y	Y	Y	Y		Y	Y
Manhattan	43,081	C	Y	Y	Y	Y	Y	Y	Y	Y	Y	Y	Y	Y
Kentucky														
Ashland	23,622	C	Y	N	Y	Y	Y	Y	Y	Y	Y		Y	Y
Fort Thomas	16,032	C	N	N	Y	Y		Y			Y	Y	Y	Y
Frankfort	25,968	C	N	Y										
Owensboro	53,549	C	N	N	N									
Paducah	27,256	C	N	N	Y									
Louisiana														
Abbeville	11,769	T	N	N	N									
Alexandria	49,188	C	Y	N	Y	Y	Y	Y	Y	Y	Y	Y	Y	Y
Baker	13,233	C	N	Y	N									
Baton Rouge	219,531	C	N	Y	Y	Y	Y	Y	Y	Y	Y	Y	Y	Y
Hammond	15,871	C	N	N										
Lafayette	101,852	C	N	N	N									
Pineville	15,308	C												
Shreveport	201,325	C												
Maine														
Auburn	24,309	C	N	N	Y	Y	Y	Y	Y	Y	Y	Y	Y	Y
Bangor	33,181	C	N	N	Y			Y	Y	Y		Y	Y	Y

State and Jurisdiction	1990 pop.	Type	Contingency plan that covers vital services in the event of a work stoppage	Legal deadline for conclusion of collective bargaining prior to budget submission	Management rights clause in any contracts	Set standards and level of service	Determine procedures and standards of selection for employment and promotion	Take disciplinary action	Relieve employees from duty with cause	Establish shifts as necessary	Determine content of job classifications	Decide whether to contract or subcontract for services	Determine missions, policies, budget, and general operations	Determine size and composition of workforce
Lewiston	39,757	C		N	Y									Y	Y
Orono	10,573	T		N	Y	Y	Y	Y	Y	Y	Y			Y	Y
Portland	64,157	C	N	N	Y		Y	Y	Y	Y			Y	Y	Y
Sanford	20,463	T	Y	N	Y										
Waterville	17,173	C	N	N	Y				Y						
Maryland															
Aberdeen	13,087	T													
Baltimore	736,014	C	Y	Y	Y	Y	Y	Y	Y					Y	Y
Bowie	37,589	C	N	N	Y		Y	Y	Y		Y	Y			
College Park	21,927	C	N	N	Y	Y	Y	Y			Y	Y	Y	Y	Y
Hagerstown	35,445	C	N	N	Y	Y	Y	Y	Y	Y				Y	Y
Rockville	44,835	C	N	N	Y	Y	Y	Y	Y	Y	Y	Y			Y
Takoma Park	16,700	C	N	N	Y	Y	Y	Y	Y		Y			Y	Y
Massachusetts															
Acton	17,872	T	N	N	Y		Y			Y		Y			
Arlington	44,630	T	N	N	Y	Y	Y		Y	Y				Y	
Ashland	12,066	T	N	N	Y	Y	Y	Y	Y	Y	Y			Y	Y
Attleboro	38,383	C	N	N	Y			Y	Y	Y		Y	Y	Y	Y
Auburn	15,005	T	N	N	Y										
Bedford	12,996	T	N	N	Y	Y	Y	Y	Y	Y		Y	Y	Y	Y

State and Jurisdiction	1990 pop.	Type	Contingency plan that covers vital services in the event of a work stoppage	Legal deadline for conclusion of collective bargaining prior to budget submission	Management rights clause in any contracts	Set standards and level of service	Determine procedures and standards of selection for employment and promotion	Take disciplinary action	Relieve employees from duty with cause	Establish shifts as necessary	Determine content of job classifications	Decide whether to contract or subcontract for services	Determine missions, policies, budget, and general operations	Determine size and composition of workforce
Bridgewater	21,249	T	N	N	Y	Y	Y	Y	Y	Y	Y	Y	Y	Y
Brookline	54,718	T	N	N	Y	Y	Y	Y	Y	Y	Y	Y	Y	Y
Cambridge	95,802	C	Y	N	Y	Y	Y	Y	Y	Y	Y	Y	Y	Y
Canton	18,530	T	N	Y	Y	Y	Y	Y	Y	Y	Y		Y	Y
Chicopee	56,632	C	N	N	Y	Y	Y	Y		Y	Y		Y	Y
Concord	17,076	T	N	N	Y	Y	Y	Y	Y		Y	Y	Y	Y
Duxbury	13,895	T	N	N	Y	Y	Y	Y	Y	Y		Y	Y	Y
East Bridgewater	11,104	T	N	N	Y	Y				Y		Y	Y	Y
Easthampton	15,537	T	Y	N	Y		Y		Y	Y	Y	Y	Y	
Easton	19,807	T	N	N	Y	Y	Y	Y	Y	Y	Y	Y	Y	Y
Franklin	22,095	T		N	Y									
Grafton	13,035	T			N									
Greenfield	18,666	T	N	N	Y	Y	Y	Y	Y	Y			Y	Y
Hanover	11,912	T	N	N	Y	Y	Y	Y	Y	Y	Y		Y	Y
Harwich	10,275	T	N	N	Y			Y	Y	Y		Y	Y	
Hingham	19,821	T	N	N	Y			Y	Y	Y			Y	
Ipswich	11,873	T	N	N	Y	Y	Y	Y	Y	Y	Y		Y	Y
Ludlow	18,820	T	N	N	Y						Y			
Lynnfield	11,274	T	N	Y	Y		Y	Y			Y			
Needham	27,557	T	N	N	Y	Y	Y	Y	Y		Y	Y	Y	Y

State and Jurisdiction	1990 pop.	Type	Contingency plan that covers vital services in the event of a work stoppage	Legal deadline for conclusion of collective bargaining prior to budget submission	Management rights clause in any contracts	Set standards and level of service	Determine procedures and standards of selection for employment and promotion	Take disciplinary action	Relieve employees from duty with cause	Establish shifts as necessary	Determine content of job classifications	Decide whether to contract or subcontract for services	Determine missions, policies, budget, and general operations	Determine size and composition of workforce
North Andover	22,792	T	N	N	Y	Y	Y	Y	Y	Y		Y	Y	
North Reading	12,002	T	N	N	Y			Y	Y				Y	
Northborough	11,929	T	Y	Y	Y	Y	Y	Y	Y		Y	Y	Y	Y
Pembroke	14,544	T	N	N	Y	Y	Y	Y	Y	Y	Y	Y	Y	Y
Plymouth	45,608	T	N	N	Y	Y	Y			Y	Y		Y	Y
Reading	22,539	T	N	N	Y	Y	Y	Y	Y		Y	Y	Y	Y
Scituate	16,786	T	Y	N	Y	Y		Y	Y	Y	Y		Y	Y
Stoneham	22,203	T			Y									
Stoughton	26,777	T	N	N	Y	Y	Y	Y	Y	Y	Y	Y	Y	Y
Tewksbury	27,266	T	N	N	Y									
Walpole	20,212	T		N	Y	Y	Y	Y	Y	Y				
Webster	16,196	T	N	N	Y	Y		Y	Y	Y			Y	
Weymouth	54,063	T	N	Y	Y	Y	Y	Y	Y		Y		Y	Y
Wilmington	17,651	T	Y	N	Y	Y	Y	Y	Y	Y	Y	Y	Y	Y
Woburn	35,943	C	N	N	Y	Y	Y	Y	Y	Y	Y	Y	Y	Y
Worcester	169,759	C	Y	N	Y	Y	Y	Y	Y	Y	Y	Y	Y	Y
Yarmouth	21,174	T	N	N	Y	Y	Y	Y	Y	Y			Y	Y
Michigan														
Adrian	22,097	C	N	N	Y	Y	Y	Y	Y	Y	Y	Y	Y	Y
Albion	10,066	C		N	Y	Y			Y				Y	

State and Jurisdiction	1990 pop.	Type	Contingency plan that covers vital services in the event of a work stoppage	Legal deadline for conclusion of collective bargaining prior to budget submission	Management rights clause in any contracts	Set standards and level of service	Determine procedures and standards of selection for employment and promotion	Take disciplinary action	Relieve employees from duty with cause	Establish shifts as necessary	Determine content of job classifications	Decide whether to contract or subcontract for services	Determine missions, policies, budget, and general operations	Determine size and composition of workforce
Allen Park	31,092	C	Y	N	Y	Y	Y		Y	Y	Y	Y	Y	Y
Alpena	11,354	C	N	N	Y	Y				Y			Y	
Ann Arbor	110,000	C	N	N	Y	Y						Y	Y	
Auburn Hills	17,076	C	Y	N	Y	Y	Y			Y	Y			Y
Bay City	38,936	C	N	N	Y	Y	Y			Y	Y	Y	Y	Y
Berkley	16,960	C	N	N	Y	Y	Y	Y	Y			Y	Y	Y
Big Rapids	12,603	C	N	N	Y	Y	Y	Y	Y	Y		Y	Y	Y
Birmingham	19,997	C	Y	N	Y	Y	Y	Y	Y	Y	Y	Y	Y	Y
Cadillac	10,104	C	N	N	Y	Y	Y	Y	Y	Y	Y	Y	Y	Y
Canton	57,040	Tp	N	N	Y	Y	Y	Y	Y	Y	Y	Y	Y	Y
East Grand Rapids	10,807	C	N	N	Y	Y		Y	Y	Y	Y		Y	Y
East Lansing	50,677	C	N	N	Y	Y	Y	Y	Y	Y	Y	Y	Y	Y
Ecorse	12,180	C	N	N	Y			Y	Y		Y	Y		Y
Escanaba	13,659	C	N	N	Y	Y	Y	Y	Y	Y	Y		Y	Y
Farmington	10,132	C	N	N	Y	Y	Y	Y	Y	Y	Y		Y	Y
Ferndale	25,084	C	N	N	Y	Y	Y	Y	Y	Y	Y	Y	Y	Y
Grand Haven	11,951	C	N	N	Y	Y	Y	Y	Y	Y	Y	Y	Y	
Grand Rapids	189,126	C	Y	N	Y	Y			Y	Y	Y		Y	

State and Jurisdiction	1990 pop.	Type	Contingency plan that covers vital services in the event of a work stoppage	Legal deadline for conclusion of collective bargaining prior to budget submission	Management rights clause in any contracts	Set standards and level of service	Determine procedures and standards of selection for employment and promotion	Take disciplinary action	Relieve employees from duty with cause	Establish shifts as necessary	Determine content of job classifications	Decide whether to contract or subcontract for services	Determine missions, policies, budget, and general operations	Determine size and composition of workforce
Harper Woods	14,903	C	N	N	Y	Y	Y	Y	Y	Y	Y		Y	Y
Jackson	37,446	C	Y	N	Y									
Kalamazoo	80,277	C	N	N	Y	Y	Y	Y	Y	Y	Y	Y	Y	Y
Kentwood	37,826	C	N	N	Y	Y	Y	Y	Y	Y	Y	Y	Y	Y
Lincoln Park	41,832	C		N	Y	Y	Y				Y			Y
Livonia	100,850	C	Y	N	Y					Y		Y	Y	Y
Marquette	21,977	C	Y	N	Y	Y	Y	Y	Y	Y	Y		Y	Y
Melvindale	11,216	C	Y	N	Y		Y	Y		Y	Y	Y		Y
Midland	38,053	C	Y	N	Y	Y				Y		Y	Y	Y
Monroe	22,902	C	Y	N	Y	Y		Y	Y				Y	Y
Mount Pleasant	23,285	C	Y	N	Y	Y	Y	Y	Y	Y	Y		Y	Y
Muskegon Heights	13,176	C	N	N	Y	Y	Y	Y	Y	Y	Y	Y	Y	Y
Niles	12,458	C	N	N	Y	Y	Y		Y	Y			Y	Y
Norton Shores	21,755	C	Y	Y		Y	Y	Y	Y	Y		Y		Y
Novi	32,998	C	Y	N	Y	Y	Y	Y	Y	Y	Y	Y	Y	Y
Oak Park	30,462	C	Y	N	Y	Y	Y	Y	Y	Y	Y	Y	Y	Y
Plainfield	24,946	Tp	Y	N	Y	Y		Y	Y	Y	Y	Y	Y	Y
Pontiac	71,166	C	Y	N	Y				Y					
Port Huron	33,694	C	Y	N	Y	Y	Y	Y	Y	Y		Y		Y

State and Jurisdiction	1990 pop.	Type	Contingency plan for event of a work stoppage	Legal deadline for conclusion of collective bargaining prior to budget submission	Management rights clause in any contracts	Set standards and level of service	Determine procedures and standards of selection for employment and promotion	Take disciplinary action	Relieve employees from duty with cause	Establish shifts as necessary	Determine content of job classifications	Decide whether to contract or subcontract for services	Determine missions, policies, budget, and general operations	Determine size and composition of workforce
Riverview	13,894	C	N	N	Y	Y				Y	Y		Y	Y
Roseville	51,412	C	N	N	Y	Y				Y	Y		Y	Y
Royal Oak	65,410	C	Y	N	Y	Y	Y	Y	Y	Y	Y	Y	Y	Y
Saginaw	69,512	C	Y	N	Y	Y	Y	Y	Y	Y	Y	Y	Y	Y
Saginaw	37,684	Tp	N	N	Y	Y	Y	Y	Y	Y	Y	Y	Y	Y
Southfield	75,728	C	Y	N	Y	Y	Y	Y	Y	Y	Y		Y	Y
Southgate	30,771	C	Y	N	Y	Y	Y	Y		Y	Y	Y	Y	Y
St. Clair Shores	68,107	C	N	N	Y		Y		Y	Y	Y	Y	Y	
Sturgis	10,130	C	N	N	Y	Y			Y	Y	Y	Y	Y	Y
Taylor	70,811	C	N	Y	N									
Traverse City	15,155	C	N	N	Y									
Trenton	20,586	C	Y	N	Y	Y	Y	Y	Y	Y	Y	Y	Y	Y
Troy	72,884	C	N	N	Y	Y	Y	Y	Y	Y	Y	Y	Y	Y
Walker	17,279	C	Y	N	Y	Y	Y	Y	Y	Y	Y	Y	Y	Y
Westland	84,724	C	Y	N	Y	Y	Y	Y	Y	Y	Y	Y	Y	Y
Wyoming	63,891	C	N	N	Y	Y	Y	Y	Y	Y	Y	Y	Y	Y
Ypsilanti	24,846	C	N	N	Y	Y	Y	Y	Y	Y	Y	Y	Y	Y
Minnesota														
Albert Lea	18,310	C	N	N	Y	Y	Y	Y		Y	Y	Y	Y	Y
Andover	15,216	C	N	N	Y	Y	Y	Y	Y	Y	Y	Y	Y	Y

State and Jurisdiction	1990 pop.	Type	Contingency plan that covers vital services in the event of a work stoppage	Legal deadline for conclusion of collective bargaining prior to budget submission	Management rights clause in any contracts	Set standards and level of service	Determine procedures and standards of selection for employment and promotion	Take disciplinary action	Relieve employees from duty with cause	Establish shifts as necessary	Determine content of job classifications	Decide whether to contract or subcontract for services	Determine missions, policies, budget, and general operations	Determine size and composition of workforce
Anoka	17,693	C	Y	N	Y	Y	Y	Y	Y	Y	Y	Y	Y	Y
Apple Valley	34,598	C		N	Y	Y				Y		Y	Y	Y
Blaine	38,975	C	Y	N	Y	Y	Y			Y	Y	Y	Y	Y
Bloomington	88,375	C	Y	N	Y	Y	Y	Y	Y	Y	Y	Y	Y	Y
Brainerd	12,353	C	N	N	Y	Y	Y	Y	Y	Y	Y		Y	Y
Brooklyn Center	28,887	C	Y	N	Y	Y	Y	Y	Y	Y	Y	Y	Y	Y
Brooklyn Park	56,381	C	Y	N	Y	Y	Y	Y	Y	Y	Y	Y	Y	Y
Crystal	23,667	C	Y	N	Y	Y	Y	Y	Y	Y	Y	Y	Y	Y
Eagan	57,757	C	Y	N	Y									
Edina	46,070	C	N	N	Y		Y	Y					Y	Y
Elk River	11,143	C	N	N	N									
Fairmont	11,265	C	Y	N	Y	Y	Y	Y	Y		Y		Y	Y
Golden Valley	20,971	C	Y	N	Y	Y	Y	Y	Y	Y	Y	Y	Y	Y
Inver Grove Heights	27,917	C	N	N	Y	Y	Y	Y	Y	Y	Y	Y	Y	Y
Lakeville	24,854	C	N	N	Y	Y	Y	Y	Y	Y	Y	Y	Y	Y
Maple Grove	38,736	C	N	N	Y	Y	Y	Y	Y	Y	Y	Y	Y	Y
Maplewood	30,954	C	N	N	Y	Y				Y		Y	Y	Y

State and Jurisdiction	1990 pop.	Type	Contingency plan that covers vital services in the event of a work stoppage	Legal deadline for conclusion of collective bargaining prior to budget submission	Management rights clause in any contracts	Set standards and level of service	Determine procedures and standards of selection for employment and promotion	Take disciplinary action	Relieve employees from duty with cause	Establish shifts as necessary	Determine content of job classifications	Decide whether to contract or subcontract for services	Determine missions, policies, budget, and general operations	Determine size and composition of workforce
Marshall	12,023	C	N	N	Y	Y	Y	Y	Y	Y	Y	Y	Y	Y
Minneapolis	358,785	C	Y	N	Y	Y	Y	Y	Y	Y	Y	Y	Y	Y
Minnetonka	52,176	C		N	Y	Y	Y	Y	Y	Y			Y	Y
Moorhead	32,295	C	Y	N	Y	Y	Y	Y	Y	Y	Y	Y	Y	Y
New Hope	21,698	C	Y	N	Y	Y	Y	Y	Y	Y	Y	Y	Y	Y
Owatonna	19,386	C	N	N	Y	Y	Y	Y	Y	Y	Y	Y	Y	
Plymouth	50,889	C	Y	N	Y	Y	Y	Y	Y	Y	Y	Y	Y	Y
Prior Lake	11,482	C	Y	N	Y	Y	Y	Y	Y	Y	Y	Y	Y	Y
Robbinsdale	14,196	C	Y	N	Y	Y	Y	Y	Y	Y	Y	Y	Y	Y
Savage	15,152	C	N	N	Y	Y	Y	Y		Y	Y	Y	Y	Y
Shakopee	11,739	C	Y	N	Y	Y	Y	Y	Y	Y	Y	Y	Y	Y
St. Louis Park	43,967	C	N	N	Y	Y	Y	Y	Y	Y	Y	Y	Y	Y
Stillwater	13,882	C	N	N	Y	Y	Y			Y	Y	Y	Y	Y
West St. Paul	19,450	C	N	N	Y	Y	Y	Y	Y	Y	Y	Y	Y	Y
White Bear Lake	24,704	C	Y	N	Y	Y	Y	Y	Y	Y	Y	Y	Y	Y
Willmar	17,531	C	Y	N	Y	Y	Y	Y	Y	Y	Y	Y	Y	
Mississippi														
Biloxi	46,319	C												
Gautier	10,088	C	Y	N	Y	Y	Y	Y	Y	Y	Y		Y	
Jackson	202,062	C												Y

State and Jurisdiction	1990 pop.	Type	Contingency plan that covers vital services in the event of a work stoppage	Legal deadline for conclusion of collective bargaining prior to budget submission	Management rights clause in any contracts	Set standards and level of service	Determine procedures and standards of selection for employment and promotion	Take disciplinary action	Relieve employees from duty with cause	Establish shifts as necessary	Determine content of job classifications	Decide whether to contract or subcontract for services	Determine missions, policies, budget, and general operations	Determine size and composition of workforce
Meridian	41,036	C	N	N	Y	Y	Y	Y	Y	Y	Y	Y	Y	Y
Moss Point	17,837	C	N	N	N									
Pascagoula	25,899	C	Y	N	Y	Y	Y	Y	Y	Y	Y	Y	Y	Y
Missouri														
Belton	18,150	C	N	N	N									
Bridgeton	17,779	C												
Cape Girardeau	34,438	C	N	N	N									
Clayton	13,874	C	Y	N										
Farmington	11,598	C	N	N	N									
Ferguson	22,286	C	N	N	Y	Y	Y	Y	Y	Y	Y	Y	Y	Y
Fulton	10,033	C	N	N	Y	Y	Y	Y	Y	Y	Y	Y	Y	Y
Gladstone	26,243	C	N	N	N									
Independence	112,301	C	N	N	Y									
Jefferson City	35,481	C	Y	N	Y	Y	Y	Y	Y	Y	Y	Y	Y	Y
Kansas City	441,259	C	Y	N	Y	Y	Y	Y	Y	Y	Y	Y	Y	Y
Kirksville	17,152	C	N	N	Y	Y	Y	Y	Y	Y		Y	Y	Y
Ofallon	18,698	C	N	N	Y	Y	Y	Y	Y		Y		Y	Y
Richmond Heights	10,448	C	N	N	N									
Rolla	14,090	C	N	N	Y									

State and Jurisdiction	1990 pop.	Type	Contingency plan that covers vital services in the event of a work stoppage	Legal deadline for conclusion of collective bargaining prior to budget submission	Management rights clause in any contracts	Set standards and level of service	Determine procedures and standards of selection for employment and promotion	Take disciplinary action	Relieve employees from duty with cause	Establish shifts as necessary	Determine content of job classifications	Decide whether to contract or subcontract for services	Determine missions, policies, budget, and general operations	Determine size and composition of workforce
Sikeston	17,641	C		N	N									
Springfield	140,494	C												
St. Joseph	71,852	C	N	N	Y	Y	Y	Y	Y	Y	Y		Y	Y
St. Louis	396,685	C	N	N	Y	Y	Y	Y	Y	Y	Y		Y	Y
University City	40,087	C	Y	N	Y	Y	Y	Y	Y	Y	Y	Y	Y	Y
Warrensburg	15,244	C	N	N	Y									
Montana														
Anaconda-Deer Lodge	10,278	C	Y	N	Y			Y	Y	Y	Y	Y	Y	
Billings	81,151	C	Y	N	Y	Y					Y	Y	Y	Y
Great Falls	55,097	C	Y	N	Y	Y					Y	Y	Y	Y
Havre	10,201	C	N		Y	Y	Y	Y	Y	Y	Y	Y	Y	Y
Nebraska														
Bellevue	39,240	C	N	N	Y	Y		Y	Y	Y				
Fremont	23,680	C	N	N	Y	Y	Y	Y	Y	Y				
Hastings	22,837	C	N	N	Y	Y		Y	Y	Y	Y			Y
Lincoln	191,972	C	N	N	Y	Y	Y	Y	Y	Y	Y	Y	Y	Y
Norfolk	21,476	C	N	N	Y	Y	Y	Y	Y	Y	Y		Y	Y
North Platte	22,605	C	N	N	Y	Y	Y			Y	Y	Y	Y	Y
Omaha	342,862	C	Y	N	Y	Y	Y					Y	Y	Y

State and Jurisdiction	1990 pop.	Type	Contingency plan for conclusion of collective bargaining in the event of a work stoppage	Legal deadline for conclusion of collective bargaining prior to budget submission	Management rights clause in any contracts	Set standards and level of service	Determine procedures and standards of selection for employment and promotion	Take disciplinary action	Relieve employees from duty with cause	Establish shifts as necessary	Determine content of job classifications	Decide whether to contract or subcontract for services	Determine missions, policies, budget, and general operations	Determine size and composition of workforce
Nevada														
Boulder City	12,567	C	Y	N	Y	Y	Y	Y	Y	Y	Y		Y	Y
Elko	14,736	C	N	N	Y		Y		Y	Y	Y		Y	Y
Henderson	64,942	C	N	N	Y	Y		Y		Y	Y		Y	Y
Las Vegas	376,906	C	N	N	Y	Y	Y	Y	Y	Y	Y			Y
North Las Vegas	47,707	C	Y	N	Y	Y	Y	Y	Y	Y	Y	Y	Y	Y
Reno	164,600	C	Y	N	Y	Y	Y	Y	Y	Y	Y	Y	Y	Y
Sparks	53,367	C	N	N	Y	Y	Y	Y			Y		Y	Y
New Hampshire														
Bedford	12,563	T	N	N	Y	Y		Y		Y			Y	
Concord	36,006	C	N	Y	Y	Y	Y	Y	Y	Y	Y	Y	Y	Y
Dover	25,042	C	N	N	Y	Y	Y	Y	Y	Y	Y	Y	Y	Y
Exeter	12,481	T	N	N	Y				Y				Y	
Keene	22,430	C	N	N	Y	Y	Y	Y	Y	Y	Y	Y	Y	Y
Manchester	99,567	C	Y	Y	Y			Y					Y	
Milford	11,795	T	Y	Y	Y	Y		Y	Y		Y		Y	Y
Rochester	26,630	C	N	N	Y	Y	Y	Y	Y	Y	Y		Y	Y
New Jersey														
Belleville	34,213	Tp	N	N	Y	Y	Y	Y		Y				Y
Branchburg	10,888	Tp	N	N	Y	Y	Y	Y	Y	Y	Y	Y	Y	Y

State and Jurisdiction	1990 pop.	Type	Contingency plan for conclusion of vital services in the event of a work stoppage	Legal deadline for conclusion of collective bargaining that covers prior to budget submission	Management rights clause in any contracts	Set standards and level of service	Determine procedures and standards of selection for employment and promotion	Take disciplinary action	Relieve employees from duty with cause	Establish shifts as necessary	Determine content of job classifications	Decide whether to contract or subcontract for services	Determine missions, policies, budget, and general operations	Determine size and composition of workforce
Brick	66,473	Tp	N	N	Y	Y	Y	Y	Y			Y	Y	Y
Clark	14,629	Tp		N	Y	Y	Y	Y	Y		Y	Y	Y	Y
Clifton	71,742	C	N	N	Y	Y	Y	Y	Y	Y	Y		Y	Y
East Brunswick	43,548	Tp	N	N	Y		Y	Y	Y	Y	Y	Y	Y	Y
Egg Harbor	23,510	Tp	Y	N	Y	Y	Y	Y	Y	Y	Y	Y	Y	Y
Evesham	35,309	Tp	N	N	Y		Y	Y	Y	Y	Y	Y		Y
Fair Lawn	30,548	B	Y	N	Y	Y	Y	Y	Y	Y	Y	Y		Y
Franklin	16,000	Tp	N	N	Y		Y	Y	Y		Y			Y
Glen Rock	10,883	B	N	N	Y		Y	Y	Y				Y	
Gloucester City	12,649	C	Y	N	Y	Y	Y	Y		Y	Y		Y	Y
Hackensack	37,049	C	Y	N	Y		Y	Y	Y	Y			Y	Y
Haddonfield	11,628	B	N	N	Y		Y	Y	Y		Y	Y	Y	Y
Highland Park	13,279	B	N	N	Y	Y	Y	Y	Y	Y	Y	Y	Y	Y
Kearny	34,874	T	N	N	Y		Y	Y				Y	Y	
Lakewood	45,048	Tp	N	N	Y	Y	Y	Y	Y	Y	Y	Y	Y	Y
Lawrence	25,787	Tp	N	N	Y	Y	Y	Y	Y	Y		Y	Y	
Lincoln Park	10,978	B	N	N	Y		Y	Y	Y	Y		Y	Y	
Lower	20,820	Tp	N	N	Y	Y	Y	Y	Y	Y	Y	Y	Y	Y
Maple Shade	19,211	Tp	Y	N	Y	Y	Y	Y	Y	Y	Y	Y	Y	Y

State and Jurisdiction	1990 pop.	Type	Contingency plan that covers vital services in the event of a work stoppage	Legal deadline for conclusion of collective bargaining prior to budget submission	Management rights clause in any contracts	Set standards and level of service	Determine procedures and standards of selection for employment and promotion	Take disciplinary action	Relieve employees from duty with cause	Establish shifts as necessary	Determine content of job classifications	Decide whether to contract or subcontract for services	Determine missions, policies, budget, and general operations	Determine size and composition of workforce
Medford	20,526	Tp	N	N	Y	Y		Y	Y	Y	Y		Y	Y
Millburn	18,630	Tp	N	N	Y	Y	Y	Y	Y	Y	Y	Y	Y	Y
Montville	15,600	Tp	Y	N	Y	Y	Y			Y				Y
Moorestown	16,116	Tp	N	N	Y	Y	Y	Y	Y	Y			Y	Y
Ocean City	15,512	C	N	N	Y								Y	Y
Old Bridge	56,475	Tp	N	N	Y	Y	Y	Y	Y				Y	Y
Passaic	58,041	C	N	N	Y	Y	Y	Y	Y	Y		Y	Y	Y
Paterson	140,891	C	N	N	Y		Y							
Phillipsburg	15,757	T	Y	N	Y	Y	Y	Y	Y	Y	Y	Y	Y	Y
Piscataway	47,089	Tp	N	N	Y	Y	Y	Y	Y		Y	Y	Y	Y
Plainsboro	14,213	Tp	N	N	Y	Y	Y	Y	Y	Y	Y	Y	Y	Y
Raritan	15,616	Tp	N	N	Y		Y	Y	Y	Y	Y		Y	Y
Ridgewood	24,152	V	N	N	Y	Y		Y	Y	Y		Y	Y	Y
Roxbury	20,429	Tp	Y	N	Y		Y	Y	Y	Y	Y	Y	Y	Y
Scotch Plains	21,160	Tp	Y	N	Y			Y	Y					
Somers Point	11,216	C	N	N	Y	Y	Y	Y	Y	Y		Y	Y	Y
South Plainfield	20,489	B	N	N	Y	Y	Y	Y	Y			Y		Y
Summit	19,757	C	N	N	Y	Y	Y	Y	Y	Y	Y	Y	Y	Y
Tenafly	13,326	B	N	Y	Y	Y	Y	Y	Y				Y	Y
Verona	13,597	Tp	N	N										Y

State and Jurisdiction	1990 pop.	Type	Contingency plan that covers vital services in the event of a work stoppage	Legal deadline for conclusion of collective bargaining prior to budget submission	Management rights clause in any contracts	Set standards and level of service	Determine procedures and standards of selection for employment and promotion	Take disciplinary action	Relieve employees from duty with cause	Establish shifts as necessary	Determine content of job classifications	Decide whether to contract or subcontract for services	Determine missions, policies, budget, and general operations	Determine size and composition of workforce
Vineland	54,780	C	N	N	Y	Y	Y	Y	Y	Y	Y	Y	Y	Y
Warren	10,830	Tp	N	N	Y		Y	Y		Y	Y	Y	Y	Y
Washington (Morris)	15,592	Tp	N	N							Y	Y	Y	Y
West Windsor	16,021	Tp	Y	N	Y	Y	Y	Y	Y	Y	Y	Y	Y	Y
Westfield	28,870	T	N	N	Y	Y		Y	Y	Y	Y	Y	Y	Y
Westwood	10,446	B	Y	N	Y									
Willingboro	36,291	Tp	Y	N	Y	Y	Y	Y		Y	Y	Y	Y	Y
Woodbridge	93,086	Tp	N	N	Y			Y	Y	Y	Y		Y	Y
New Mexico														
Albuquerque	419,681	C	N	N	N									
Artesia	10,610	C	N	N		Y	Y	Y	Y	Y	Y		Y	Y
Clovis	30,954	C	Y	N	Y	Y	Y	Y	Y	Y	Y	Y	Y	Y
Deming	11,422	C	N	N	Y	Y	Y	Y	Y	Y	Y		Y	Y
Las Cruces	62,126	C	N	N	Y	Y	Y	Y	Y	Y	Y	Y	Y	Y
Portales	10,690	C	N	Y	Y	Y	Y	Y	Y	Y			Y	Y
Rio Rancho	32,505	C	N	N	Y	Y	Y	Y	Y		Y		Y	Y
New York														
Auburn	31,258	C	N	Y	Y	Y	Y	Y	Y		Y			
Beacon	13,243	C	N	N	Y	Y	Y	Y	Y		Y	Y	Y	
Buffalo	328,123	C	Y	N	Y	Y	Y	Y			Y		Y	Y

State and Jurisdiction	1990 pop.	Type	Contingency plan that covers vital services in the event of a work stoppage	Legal deadline for conclusion of collective bargaining prior to budget submission	Management rights clause in any contracts	Set standards and level of service	Determine procedures and standards of selection for employment and promotion	Take disciplinary action	Relieve employees from duty with cause	Establish shifts as necessary	Determine content of job classifications	Decide whether to contract or subcontract for services	Determine missions, policies, budget, and general operations	Determine size and composition of workforce
Cortland	19,801	C	N	N	Y	Y	Y	Y	Y		Y	Y	Y	Y
Cortlandt	37,357	T	N	N	Y				Y		Y	Y	Y	
East Rockaway	10,152	V	N	N	N									
Elmira	32,009	C	N	N	Y	Y								
Garden City	21,686	V	Y	N	Y	Y	Y	Y	Y	Y	Y	Y	Y	Y
Geneva	13,890	C	N	N	Y	Y	Y	Y	Y	Y	Y	Y	Y	Y
Hamburg	10,442	V	N	N	Y	Y	Y	Y	Y				Y	Y
Harrison	23,308	V	Y	N				Y	Y		Y		Y	Y
Ithaca	29,541	C	N	N	Y	Y	Y	Y	Y	Y	Y		Y	Y
Jamestown	34,681	C	N	N	Y	Y	Y	Y	Y	Y	Y		Y	Y
Johnson City	16,890	V	Y	N	Y		Y						Y	
Lindenhurst	26,879	V	N	N	Y			Y		Y				
Mamaroneck	17,325	T	Y	N	Y		Y			Y	Y		Y	Y
Mamaroneck	10,294	V	N	N	Y	Y				Y	Y		Y	Y
New Rochelle	67,265	C	N	N	Y	Y	Y	Y	Y	Y	Y		Y	Y
Newburgh	26,454	C	N	N	Y	Y	Y	Y	Y	Y	Y	Y	Y	Y
Ogdensburg	12,993	C	N	N	Y	Y			Y	Y	Y		Y	Y
Oneonta	13,954	C	N	Y	Y	Y	Y	Y	Y	Y	Y	Y	Y	Y
Ossining	22,582	V	N	N	Y	Y		Y	Y	Y	Y	Y		Y

State and Jurisdiction	1990 pop.	Type	Contingency plan for covers sion of vital services in the event of a work stoppage	Legal deadline for conclusion of collective bargaining prior to budget submission	Management rights clause in any contracts	Set standards and level of service	Determine procedures and standards of selection for employment and promotion	Take disciplinary action	Relieve employees from duty with cause	Establish shifts as necessary	Determine content of job classifications	Decide whether to contract or subcontract for services	Determine missions, policies, budget, and general operations	Determine size and composition of workforce
Potsdam	10,251	V	N	N	Y	Y	Y	Y	Y					Y
Scarsdale	16,987	V	Y	N	Y	Y	Y	Y	Y			Y	Y	Y
Suffern	11,055	V	N	N	Y			Y	Y	Y	Y	Y	Y	Y
Syracuse	163,860	C	Y	N	Y	Y	Y	Y	Y	Y	Y	Y	Y	Y
Tarrytown	10,739	V	N	N	N									
Troy	54,269	C	N	N										
Westbury	13,060	V	N	N	Y	Y	Y	Y	Y	Y			Y	Y
North Carolina														
Albemarle	14,939	C	N											
Chapel Hill	38,719	T	N	N	N									
Charlotte	419,539	C	Y											
Concord	29,591	C	N											
Durham	138,894	C	Y	N	N									
Elizabeth City	16,087	C	N	N										
Garner	14,967	T	Y											
Gastonia	54,732	C	N											
Greensboro	183,521	C	N											
Hickory	28,301	C	N	N	N									
Kernersville	11,860	T	N	N	N									
Lenoir	16,337	C												
Raleigh	207,951	C	Y											

State and Jurisdiction	1990 pop.	Type	Contingency plan that covers vital services in the event of a work stoppage	Legal deadline for conclusion of collective bargaining prior to budget submission	Management rights clause in any contracts	Set standards and level of service	Determine procedures and standards of selection for employment and promotion	Take disciplinary action	Relieve employees from duty with cause	Establish shifts as necessary	Determine content of job classifications	Decide whether to contract or subcontract for services	Determine missions, policies, budget, and general operations	Determine size and composition of workforce
Sanford	18,887	C	N	N	N									
Statesville	20,647	C	N	N	N									
North Dakota														
Dickinson	16,097	C	N		N									
Minot	34,544	C	Y											
Ohio														
Akron	223,019	C	Y	N	Y	Y	Y	Y	Y		Y	Y	Y	Y
Avon Lake	15,066	C	Y	Y	Y	Y	Y	Y		Y	Y	Y	Y	Y
Beachwood	10,677	C	N	N	Y	Y	Y	Y	Y	Y	Y	Y	Y	Y
Bedford Heights	12,131	C	N	N	Y	Y	Y	Y	Y	Y	Y	Y	Y	Y
Bellefontaine	12,142	C	Y	Y	Y	Y	Y	Y	Y	Y	Y	Y	Y	Y
Blue Ash	11,860	C	N	N	Y	Y	Y	Y	Y	Y	Y	Y	Y	Y
Bowling Green	28,176	C	Y	N	Y	Y	Y	Y	Y	Y	Y	Y	Y	Y
Broadview Heights	12,219	C	Y	N	Y	Y	Y	Y	Y	Y	Y	Y	Y	Y
Brunswick	28,230	C	Y	N	Y	Y	Y	Y	Y	Y	Y	Y	Y	Y
Cambridge	11,748	C	Y	N	Y	Y	Y	Y	Y	Y	Y	Y	Y	Y
Canton	84,161	C	N	N	Y	Y	Y	Y	Y	Y	Y	Y	Y	Y
Circleville	11,666	C	Y	N	Y	Y	Y	Y	Y	Y	Y	Y	Y	Y

State and Jurisdiction	1990 pop.	Type	Contingency plan that covers vital services in the event of a work stoppage	Legal deadline for conclusion of collective bargaining prior to budget submission	Management rights clause in any contracts	Set standards and level of service	Determine procedures and standards of selection for employment and promotion	Take disciplinary action	Relieve employees from duty with cause	Establish shifts as necessary	Determine content of job classifications	Decide whether to contract or subcontract for services	Determine missions, policies, budget, and general operations	Determine size and composition of workforce
Cleveland Heights	54,052	C	N	N	Y	Y	Y		Y		Y		Y	Y
Colerain Township	62,000	T	N	N	Y	Y	Y		Y	Y	Y		Y	Y
Columbus	632,910	C	Y	N	Y									
Conneaut	13,241	C	N	N	Y	Y	Y	Y	Y					Y
Dayton	172,947	C	Y	N	Y	Y	Y	Y	Y	Y	Y	Y	Y	Y
Delhi	30,250	Tp	N	N	Y	Y	Y	Y	Y	Y	Y	Y	Y	Y
Fairborn	31,300	C	Y	N	Y	Y							Y	Y
Forest Park	18,609	C	N	N	Y	Y	Y	Y	Y	Y		Y	Y	Y
Gahanna	27,791	C	N	N	Y	Y	Y	Y	Y	Y	Y	Y	Y	Y
Galion	11,859	C	N	N	Y	Y	Y	Y	Y	Y	Y		Y	Y
Garfield Heights	31,739	C	Y	N	Y	Y	Y	Y	Y	Y	Y	Y	Y	Y
Hamilton	61,368	C	Y	N	Y	Y		Y		Y			Y	Y
Kettering	60,569	C	N	N	Y	Y	Y	Y	Y	Y	Y	Y	Y	Y
Lebanon	10,453	C		N	Y	Y	Y	Y	Y	Y	Y	Y	Y	Y
Lima	45,549	C	Y	N	Y	Y	Y		Y	Y	Y		Y	Y
Marietta	15,026	C	N	N	Y	Y	Y	Y	Y	Y	Y	Y	Y	Y
Marion	34,075	C	N	N	Y	Y	Y	Y	Y	Y	Y		Y	Y
Mason	11,452	C	N	N	Y	Y	Y	Y	Y	Y	Y	Y	Y	Y
Miami	28,199	Tp	N	N	Y	Y	Y	Y	Y	Y	Y		Y	Y
Miamisburg	17,834	C	Y	N	Y	Y	Y	Y	Y	Y	Y	Y	Y	Y

State and Jurisdiction	1990 pop.	Type	Contingency plan that covers vital services in the event of a work stoppage	Legal deadline for conclusion of collective bargaining prior to budget submission	Management rights clause in any contracts	Set standards and level of service	Determine procedures and standards of selection for employment and promotion	Take disciplinary action	Relieve employees from duty with cause	Establish shifts as necessary	Determine content of job classifications	Decide whether to contract or subcontract for services	Determine missions, policies, budget, and general operations	Determine size and composition of workforce
Middletown	46,022	C	Y	N	Y	Y	Y	Y	Y	Y	Y	Y	Y	Y
Mount Vernon	14,550	C	N	N	Y	Y	Y	Y	Y	Y	Y	Y	Y	Y
North College Hill	11,002	C	N	N	Y	Y	Y	Y		Y			Y	
North Olmsted	34,204	C	Y	N	N									
Oregon	18,334	C	Y	Y	Y	Y	Y	Y	Y	Y	Y	Y	Y	Y
Oxford	18,937	C	Y	N	Y	Y	Y	Y	Y	Y	Y	Y	Y	Y
Painesville	15,699	C	N	N	Y	Y	Y	Y	Y	Y		Y	Y	Y
Reading	12,038	C	Y	N	Y	Y	Y	Y	Y	Y	Y		Y	
Sandusky	29,764	C	Y	N	Y	Y	Y	Y	Y	Y	Y	Y	Y	Y
Sidney	18,710	C	Y	N	Y	Y	Y	Y	Y	Y	Y	Y	Y	Y
Springfield	70,487	C	Y	N	Y	Y	Y	Y	Y		Y	Y	Y	Y
Springfield	13,352	Tp	N	N	Y	Y	Y	Y	Y	Y	Y	Y	Y	Y
Steubenville	22,125	C	Y	N	Y								Y	Y
Stow	27,702	C	N	N	Y	Y	Y	Y	Y	Y	Y	Y	Y	Y
Strongsville	35,308	C		N	Y	Y	Y	Y	Y	Y	Y		Y	Y
Struthers	12,284	C	Y	Y	N									
Sylvania	17,301	C	Y	N	Y	Y	Y	Y	Y	Y	Y	Y	Y	Y
Tiffin	18,604	C	N	N	Y	Y	Y	Y	Y	Y	Y	Y	Y	Y
Troy	19,478	C	Y	N	Y	Y	Y	Y	Y	Y	Y	Y	Y	Y
Union	39,703	Tp	N	N	Y	Y	Y	Y	Y	Y				Y

State and Jurisdiction	1990 pop.	Type	Contingency plan that covers vital services in the event of a work stoppage	Legal deadline for conclusion of collective bargaining prior to budget submission	Management rights clause in any contracts	Set standards and level of service	Determine procedures and standards of selection for employment and promotion	Take disciplinary action	Relieve employees from duty with cause	Establish shifts as necessary	Determine content of job classifications	Decide whether to contract or subcontract for services	Determine missions, policies, budget, and general operations	Determine size and composition of workforce
University Heights	14,790	C	Y	N	Y	Y	Y	Y	Y	Y	Y	Y	Y	Y
Upper Arlington	34,128	C	N	N	Y	Y	Y	Y	Y	Y	Y	Y	Y	Y
Vandalia	13,882	C	Y	N	Y	Y	Y	Y	Y	Y	Y	Y	Y	Y
Vermilion	11,127	C	Y	N	Y	Y		Y	Y		Y	Y		Y
Warrensville Heights	15,884	C	Y	Y	Y									
Washington	12,983	C	N	N	Y	Y		Y	Y	Y	Y			Y
West Carrollton	14,403	C	Y	N	Y	Y	Y	Y	Y		Y		Y	Y
Westerville	30,269	C			Y	Y	Y	Y				Y	Y	Y
Willoughby	20,510	C	N	N	Y	Y	Y	Y	Y	Y	Y	Y	Y	Y
Wooster	22,191	C	Y	N	Y	Y	Y	Y	Y	Y	Y	Y	Y	Y
Worthington	14,869	C	N	N	Y	Y	Y	Y	Y		Y	Y	Y	Y
Xenia	24,664	C	Y	N	Y	Y	Y	Y	Y	Y	Y	Y		Y
Zanesville	26,778	C	N	N	Y	Y	Y	Y	Y	Y			Y	Y
Oklahoma														
Ada	15,820	C	N	N	Y									
Ardmore	23,079	C	N	N	Y	Y		Y	Y	Y	Y		Y	Y
Bartlesville	34,256	C	N	N	Y	Y	Y	Y	Y	Y	Y		Y	Y
Bethany	20,075	C	N	Y	Y	Y	Y	Y	Y	Y	Y	Y	Y	Y

State and Jurisdiction	1990 pop.	Type	Contingency plan that covers vital services in the event of a work stoppage	Legal deadline for conclusion of collective bargaining prior to budget submission	Management rights clause in any contracts	Set standards and level of service	Determine procedures and standards of selection for employment and promotion	Take disciplinary action	Relieve employees from duty with cause	Establish shifts as necessary	Determine content of job classifications	Decide whether to contract or subcontract for services	Determine missions, policies, budget, and general operations	Determine size and composition of workforce
Broken Arrow	58,043	C	N	N	Y	Y	Y	Y	Y	Y	Y		Y	Y
Chickasha	14,988	C	N	Y	Y	Y	Y	Y	Y	Y	Y		Y	
Claremore	13,280	C	N	N	Y		Y	Y	Y	Y	Y		Y	Y
Duncan	21,732	C	N	N	Y	Y	Y	Y	Y	Y	Y		Y	Y
Durant	12,823	C	Y	N	Y		Y	Y	Y	Y	Y	Y	Y	Y
Edmond	52,315	C	Y	Y	Y	Y	Y	Y	Y	Y	Y	Y	Y	Y
El Reno	15,414	C	N	N	Y	Y					Y		Y	Y
Guthrie	10,518	C	N	Y	Y	Y	Y	Y		Y	Y		Y	Y
Midwest City	52,267	C	N	N	Y	Y	Y	Y	Y	Y	Y		Y	Y
Norman	80,071	C	N	N	Y	Y	Y	Y	Y	Y	Y		Y	Y
Oklahoma City	469,852	C	N	N	Y	Y		Y	Y			Y		
Okmulgee	13,441	C	Y	N	Y		Y	Y		Y			Y	
Owasso	11,151	C	N	N	Y		Y	Y	Y				Y	
Ponca City	26,359	C	N	N	Y	Y	Y	Y	Y	Y			Y	Y
Sand Springs	15,346	C	N	N	Y	Y	Y	Y	Y	Y	Y	Y	Y	Y
Shawnee	26,017	C	N	N	Y	Y	Y	Y		Y	Y		Y	Y
Woodward	12,340	C	N	Y	Y	Y	Y	Y	Y	Y	Y	Y	Y	Y
Yukon	20,935	C	Y	N	Y				Y				Y	Y

Oregon

State and Jurisdiction	1990 pop.	Type	Contingency plan that covers vital services in the event of a work stoppage	Legal deadline for conclusion of collective bargaining prior to budget submission	Management rights clause in any contracts	Set standards and level of service	Determine procedures and standards of selection for employment and promotion	Take disciplinary action	Relieve employees from duty with cause	Establish shifts as necessary	Determine content of job classifications	Decide whether to contract or subcontract for services	Determine missions, policies, budget, and general operations	Determine size and composition of workforce
Albany	33,523	C	Y	N	Y	Y	Y	Y	Y	Y	Y	Y	Y	Y
Astoria	10,069	C	N	N	Y	Y	Y	Y	Y	Y	Y	Y	Y	Y
Bend	23,740	C	N	N	Y	Y	Y	Y	Y				Y	Y
Coos Bay	15,076	C	N	N	Y	Y		Y	Y	Y	Y	Y	Y	Y
Eugene	133,000	C	Y	N	Y	Y	Y	Y	Y	Y	Y	Y	Y	Y
Forest Grove	13,559	C	Y	N	Y	Y	Y	Y	Y	Y	Y	Y	Y	Y
Gladstone	10,152	C	N	N	Y	Y	Y	Y	Y	Y	Y	Y	Y	Y
Grants Pass	17,488	C	Y	N	Y	Y			Y	Y			Y	Y
Gresham	81,865	C	Y	N	Y	Y	Y	Y	Y	Y	Y		Y	
Hermiston	10,040	C	N	N	Y		Y	Y	Y	Y	Y		Y	Y
La Grande	11,766	C	N	N	Y	Y	Y	Y	Y	Y	Y	Y	Y	Y
Lebanon	10,950	C	N	N	Y	Y	Y	Y	Y	Y	Y	Y	Y	Y
Medford	46,951	C	N	N	Y	Y	Y	Y		Y			Y	
Milwaukie	18,692	C	N	N	Y	Y	Y	Y	Y	Y	Y	Y	Y	Y
Newberg	13,086	C	N	N	Y	Y	Y	Y	Y	Y	Y	Y	Y	Y
Pendleton	15,126	C	N	N	Y	Y	Y	Y	Y	Y	Y		Y	Y
Roseburg	18,389	C	Y	N	Y	Y	Y	Y	Y	Y	Y	Y	Y	Y
Salem	107,786	C	Y	N	Y	Y	Y	Y	Y	Y	Y	Y	Y	Y
Springfield	44,683	C	N	N	Y	Y	Y	Y	Y				Y	Y
The Dalles	11,060	C	Y	N	Y	Y	Y		Y		Y		Y	

State and Jurisdiction	1990 pop.	Type	Contingency plan that covers vital services in the event of a work stoppage	Legal deadline for conclusion of collective bargaining prior to budget submission	Management rights clause in any contracts	Set standards and level of service	Determine procedures and standards of selection for employment and promotion	Take disciplinary action	Relieve employees from duty with cause	Establish shifts as necessary	Determine content of job classifications	Decide whether to contract or subcontract for services	Determine missions, policies, budget, and general operations	Determine size and composition of workforce
Tigard	29,344	C	N	N	Y	Y	Y	Y	Y	Y	Y	Y	Y	Y
Tualatin	15,013	C	Y	N	Y	Y	Y	Y	Y	Y	Y	Y	Y	Y
West Linn	21,405	C	N	N	Y									
Woodburn	13,404	C	N	N	Y	Y	Y	Y	Y	Y	Y	Y	Y	Y
Pennsylvania														
Abington	56,322	Tp	N	Y	Y	Y	Y	Y	Y	Y	Y	Y	Y	Y
Altoona	51,881	C	N	N	Y	Y	Y	Y	Y	Y	Y			
Aston	15,080	Tp	N	N	N									
Beaver Falls	10,687	C	N	Y	Y	Y	Y	Y	Y	Y	Y		Y	Y
Berwick	10,976	B	N	N	Y	Y	Y	Y	Y	Y	Y	Y	Y	Y
Bethlehem	71,428	C	Y	N	Y	Y	Y	Y			Y	Y	Y	Y
Carbondale	10,664	C	Y	N	Y	Y	Y	Y	Y	Y	Y	Y	Y	Y
Chambersburg	16,647	B	Y	N	Y	Y	Y	Y	Y	Y	Y	Y	Y	Y
Coatesville	11,038	C	N	N	Y		Y	Y	Y				Y	Y
Cranberry	14,816	Tp	Y	N	Y	Y	Y	Y	Y	Y	Y		Y	Y
Darby	10,955	Tp	N	N	Y			Y						
Erie	108,718	C		N	Y			Y						
Fairview Township	13,258	Tp	N	N	Y	Y		Y	Y	Y				Y
Franklin Park	10,109	B	N	N	Y	Y	Y	Y	Y	Y			Y	Y
Greensburg	16,318	C	Y	N	Y	Y	Y	Y	Y	Y	Y	Y	Y	Y

State and Jurisdiction	1990 pop.	Type	Contingency plan that covers vital services in the event of a work stoppage	Legal deadline for conclusion of collective bargaining prior to budget submission	Management rights clause in any contracts	Set standards and level of service	Determine procedures and standards of selection for employment and promotion	Take disciplinary action	Relieve employees from duty with cause	Establish shifts as necessary	Determine content of job classifications	Decide whether to contract or subcontract for services	Determine missions, policies, budget, and general operations	Determine size and composition of workforce
Hanover	14,399	B	N	Y	Y	Y	Y			Y				Y
Harrison	11,763	Tp	N	N	Y	Y								Y
Haverford	49,848	Tp	N	N	Y	Y	Y	Y	Y	Y	Y	Y	Y	Y
Hempfield	42,609	Tp	N	N	Y			Y			Y			
Horsham	21,896	Tp	N	N	Y			Y	Y	Y				
Johnstown	28,134	C	Y	N	Y	Y	Y	Y	Y	Y	Y	Y	Y	Y
Lancaster	55,551	C	Y	Y	Y	Y	Y	Y	Y	Y			Y	Y
Lansdowne	11,712	B	Y	Y	Y			Y	Y	Y				
Lower Allen	15,254	Tp	N	N	Y	Y	Y	Y	Y	Y	Y		Y	Y
Lower Burrell	12,251	C	N	Y	Y	Y		Y	Y	Y	Y		Y	Y
Lower Paxton	39,162	Tp	Y	Y	Y		Y	Y	Y	Y			Y	Y
Lower Southampton	19,860	Tp	N	N	Y	Y	Y	Y	Y	Y	Y	Y	Y	Y
Manheim	28,880	Tp	N	N	Y	Y	Y	Y	Y	Y	Y	Y	Y	Y
McCandless	28,781	T	Y	N	Y			Y	Y	Y				
Monroeville	29,169	B	N	N	Y	Y	Y	Y	Y				Y	Y
Montgomery	12,179	Tp	N	N	N									
Mount Lebanon	33,362	C	N	N	Y	Y	Y	Y	Y	Y	Y	Y	Y	Y
Newtown Township	13,685	Tp	Y	N	Y				Y					Y

State and Jurisdiction	1990 pop.	Type	Contingency plan that covers vital services in the event of a work stoppage	Legal deadline for conclusion of collective bargaining prior to budget submission	Management rights clause in any contracts	Set standards and level of service	Determine procedures and standards of selection for employment and promotion	Take disciplinary action	Relieve employees from duty with cause	Establish shifts as necessary	Determine content of job classifications	Decide whether to contract or subcontract for services	Determine missions, policies, budget, and general operations	Determine size and composition of workforce
Newtown	11,366	Tp	N	N	N	Y	Y	Y	Y	Y	Y		Y	Y
North Huntingdon	28,158	Tp	N	Y	Y			Y	Y	Y		Y	Y	Y
Northampton	35,406	Tp	Y	N	Y		Y	Y	Y		Y	Y	Y	Y
Oil City	11,949	C	Y	N	Y		Y	Y	Y	Y			Y	
Penn Hills	51,479	C	Y	Y	Y	Y	Y	Y	Y		Y	Y	Y	Y
Philadelphia	1,585,577	C		Y	Y	Y	Y	Y	Y	Y	Y		Y	Y
Plum	25,609	B	Y	N	Y		Y	Y	Y	Y			Y	Y
Radnor	28,703	Tp	Y	N	Y	Y	Y	Y	Y	Y	Y		Y	Y
Reading	78,380	C	Y	Y	Y	Y	Y	Y	Y	Y	Y	Y	Y	Y
Richland	12,777	Tp	N	N	Y	Y	Y	Y	Y		Y		Y	Y
Ridley	31,169	Tp	N	Y	Y	Y	Y	Y	Y		Y		Y	Y
Robinson	10,830	Tp	Y	N	Y				Y	Y	Y			
Ross	33,482	Tp	N	N	Y	Y		Y	Y	Y	Y	Y		
Shaler	30,533	Tp	Y	Y	Y	Y	Y	Y	Y	Y	Y	Y	Y	Y
Sharon	17,493	C	Y	N	Y	Y							Y	
South Fayette	10,329	Tp	N	N	Y	Y		Y	Y	Y	Y	Y	Y	
Spring Garden	11,207	Tp	Y		Y		Y						Y	
Spring	18,899	Tp	N	Y	Y	Y	Y	Y	Y	Y	Y		Y	Y
Springettsbury	21,564	Tp	Y	Y	Y	Y	Y	Y	Y	Y	Y		Y	Y

State and Jurisdiction	1990 pop.	Type	Contingency plan that covers vital services in the event of a work stoppage	Legal deadline for conclusion of collective bargaining prior to budget submission	Management rights clause in any contracts	Set standards and level of service	Determine procedures and standards of selection for employment and promotion	Take disciplinary action	Relieve employees from duty with cause	Establish shifts as necessary	Determine content of job classifications	Decide whether to contract or subcontract for services	Determine missions, policies, budget, and general operations	Determine size and composition of workforce
Springfield	19,612	Tp	Y	N	N									
St. Marys	14,020	B	N	N	Y	Y			Y				Y	Y
Swatara	19,661	Tp	N	Y	N	Y								Y
Upper Gwynedd	12,197	Tp	N	N	Y	Y	Y	Y	Y	Y	Y	Y	Y	Y
Upper Merion	25,722	Tp	Y	Y	Y	Y	Y	Y	Y	Y			Y	Y
Upper St. Clair	19,692	Tp	Y	N	Y	Y	Y	Y	Y	Y	Y	Y	Y	Y
Uwchlan	12,999	Tp	N	N	Y	Y	Y	Y	Y	Y	Y	Y	Y	Y
Warwick	11,622	Tp	N	N	Y	Y	Y	Y	Y		Y	Y	Y	Y
West Chester	18,041	B	N	N	Y	Y	Y	Y	Y	Y		Y	Y	Y
West Goshen	18,082	Tp	N	N	Y			Y						
West Mifflin	23,644	B	Y	N	Y	Y	Y	Y	Y	Y	Y		Y	Y
West Whiteland	12,403	Tp	N	Y	Y		Y	Y	Y	Y	Y		Y	Y
Whitehall	14,451	B				Y								
Whitehall	22,779	Tp	Y	Y	Y	Y	Y	Y		Y		Y	Y	
Whitemarsh	14,863	Tp	N	N	Y	Y	Y	Y			Y		Y	Y
York	42,192	C	Y	N	Y	Y	Y	Y	Y	Y	Y		Y	Y
York	19,231	Tp	N	N	Y		Y	Y	Y	Y		Y	Y	Y

State and Jurisdiction	1990 pop.	Type	Contingency plan that covers vital services in the event of a work stoppage	Legal deadline for conclusion of collective bargaining prior to budget submission	Management rights clause in any contracts	Set standards and level of service	Determine procedures and standards of selection for employment and promotion	Take disciplinary action	Relieve employees from duty with cause	Establish shifts as necessary	Determine content of job classifications	Decide whether to contract or subcontract for services	Determine missions, policies, budget, and general operations	Determine size and composition of workforce
Rhode Island														
Bristol	21,625	T	N	N	Y		Y				Y		Y	
Coventry	31,083	T	N	Y	Y	Y	Y	Y	Y	Y	Y	Y	Y	Y
Cumberland	29,038	T	N	N	Y	Y	Y	Y	Y	Y			Y	Y
Lincoln	18,045	T	N	Y	Y	Y	Y	Y	Y				Y	Y
Narragansett	14,985	T	N	N	Y		Y	Y	Y	Y				Y
North Kingstown	23,786	T	N	N	Y									
North Smithfield	10,497	T	N	N	Y	Y	Y	Y	Y					
Portsmouth	16,857	T	Y	N	Y	Y	Y	Y	Y		Y		Y	Y
Smithfield	19,163	T	N	N	Y		Y	Y	Y	Y				
Warren	11,385	T	N	N	Y	Y	Y	Y	Y		Y			
South Carolina														
North Charleston	70,218	C	N											
South Dakota														
Aberdeen	24,927	C	N	N										Y
Huron	12,448	C	N	N	Y		Y	Y	Y	Y	Y	Y	Y	Y
Pierre	12,906	C	N	N	Y	Y	Y	Y	Y	Y	Y	Y		Y
Rapid City	54,523	C	Y	N	Y	Y		Y	Y	Y	Y	Y	Y	Y
Vermillion	10,034	C	N	N	Y		Y	Y	Y	Y	Y		Y	Y
Watertown	17,592	C	N	N	Y	Y	Y	Y	Y	Y	Y	Y	Y	Y

State and Jurisdiction	1990 pop.	Type	Contingency plan that covers vital services in the event of a work stoppage	Legal deadline for conclusion of collective bargaining prior to budget submission	Management rights clause in any contracts	Set standards and level of service	Determine procedures and standards of selection for employment and promotion	Take disciplinary action	Relieve employees from duty with cause	Establish shifts as necessary	Determine content of job classifications	Decide whether to contract or subcontract for services	Determine missions, policies, budget, and general operations	Determine size and composition of workforce
Tennessee														
Bartlett	26,989	T	Y											
Germantown	32,893	C												
Millington	17,866	C	Y	N										
Texas														
Amarillo	157,615	C	N	N	N									
Austin	567,566	C		N	Y	Y	Y	Y						
Balch Springs	17,406	C						Y			Y		Y	Y
Big Spring	23,093	C	N	N										
Brownsville	107,027	C	N	N	Y	Y		Y	Y	Y			Y	Y
Colleyville	12,724	C	N	N	N			Y	Y					
Corpus Christi	257,453	C	N	N	Y		Y	Y	Y					
Denton	73,483	C	N	N										
Euless	38,149	C	N	N										
Fort Worth	484,502	C	N	N										
Gainesville	14,256	C	Y	N	N									
Greenville	23,071	C	N	N										
Haltom City	32,856	C	N		N									
Harlingen	48,735	C	N	N	N									
Hurst	33,574	C	N	N	N									

State and Jurisdiction	1990 pop.	Type	Contingency plan for conclusion of a work stoppage	Legal deadline for conclusion of collective bargaining prior to budget submission	Management rights clause in any contracts	Set standards and level of service	Determine procedures and standards of selection for employment and promotion	Take disciplinary action	Relieve employees from duty with cause	Establish shifts as necessary	Determine content of job classifications	Decide whether to contract or subcontract for services	Determine missions, policies, budget, and general operations	Determine size and composition of workforce
Kingsville	25,276	C	Y	Y	Y	Y	Y	Y	Y		Y		Y	Y
La Marque	14,120	C	N	N	Y	Y	Y	Y	Y	Y	Y		Y	Y
Lancaster	22,117	C	N	N	N									
League City	30,159	C	N	N	N									
Lewisville	46,521	C	N		N									
Longview	70,311	C	N	N	N									
Lubbock	193,679	C												
Mansfield	15,607	C	N	N	N									
Mc Allen	84,021	C	N	N										
Mesquite	101,484	C	N	N	N									
Missouri City	36,176	C	N	N										
Nederland	16,192	C	Y	N	Y									
New Braunfels	27,334	C	N	N										
Palestine	18,042	C	N	N	N									
Plainview	21,700	C	N	N	Y	Y								
Port Arthur	58,724	C	N	N	Y	Y				Y	Y		Y	Y
Port Neches	12,974	C	N	N	Y	Y		Y	Y	Y	Y		Y	Y
San Antonio	1,115,600	C		N	Y	Y		Y	Y	Y	Y	Y	Y	Y
San Juan	12,561	C	N	N	N									
Sherman	31,601	C	N	N										

State and Jurisdiction	1990 pop.	Type	Contingency plan that covers vital services in the event of a work stoppage	Legal deadline for conclusion of collective bargaining prior to budget submission	Management rights clause in any contracts	Set standards and level of service	Determine procedures and standards of selection for employment and promotion	Take disciplinary action	Relieve employees from duty with cause	Establish shifts as necessary	Determine content of job classifications	Decide whether to contract or subcontract for services	Determine missions, policies, budget, and general operations	Determine size and composition of workforce
University Park	22,259	C	N	N	N									
Vidor	10,935	C	N	N	Y	Y	Y	Y	Y	Y	Y	Y	Y	Y
Waxahachie	18,168	C	N											
Wichita Falls	96,259	C	Y	N	N									
Utah														
Ogden City	63,909	C	Y	N	N									
Provo	86,835	C	N	N	N									
South Jordan	12,220	C	N	N	N									
Vermont														
Bennington	16,451	T	N	N	Y	Y	Y	Y	Y	Y	Y	Y	Y	Y
Colchester	14,731	T	N	N	Y		Y	Y	Y	Y	Y		Y	Y
Essex	16,498	T	N	N	Y								Y	
Virginia														
Alexandria	111,183	C												
Chesapeake	151,976	C	N											
Portsmouth	103,907	C	N	N										
Roanoke	96,397	C	N											
Salem	23,756	C												
Washington														
Anacortes	11,451	C	N	N	Y		Y					Y	Y	Y

State and Jurisdiction	1990 pop.	Type	Contingency plan that covers vital services in the event of a work stoppage	Legal deadline for conclusion of collective bargaining prior to budget submission	Management rights clause in any contracts	Set standards and level of service	Determine procedures and standards of selection for employment and promotion	Take disciplinary action	Relieve employees from duty with cause	Establish shifts as necessary	Determine content of job classifications	Decide whether to contract or subcontract for services	Determine missions, policies, budget, and general operations	Determine size and composition of workforce
Centralia	12,101	C	N	N	Y	Y								
Des Moines	17,283	C	N	N	Y	Y	Y	Y	Y	Y	Y	Y	Y	Y
Edmonds	30,744	C	N	N	Y	Y	Y		Y	Y	Y		Y	Y
Ellensburg	12,361	C	Y	N	Y	Y	Y		Y				Y	Y
Federal Way	67,535	C	N	N	Y							Y	Y	Y
Kelso	11,820	C	Y	N	Y	Y			Y	Y	Y		Y	Y
Kennewick	42,155	C	N	N	Y	Y		Y	Y	Y	Y		Y	Y
Kent	37,960	C	N	N	Y	Y	Y	Y	Y	Y	Y		Y	Y
Lacey	19,279	C	N	N	Y	Y	Y	Y	Y	Y	Y	Y	Y	Y
Lakewood	58,412	C	N	N	N									
Marysville	11,575	C	Y	N	Y	Y	Y	Y	Y	Y	Y	Y	Y	Y
Mercer Island	20,816	C	N	N	Y	Y	Y	Y	Y	Y	Y	Y	Y	Y
Mountlake Terrace	19,320	C	N	N	Y	Y	Y	Y	Y		Y	Y	Y	Y
Olympia	33,840	C	N	N	Y	Y	Y	Y	Y	Y	Y	Y	Y	Y
Pasco	20,337	C	N	N	Y	Y	Y		Y		Y		Y	Y
Pullman	23,478	C	N	N	Y									
Redmond	35,800	C	N	N	Y	Y	Y	Y	Y	Y	Y		Y	Y
Renton	41,688	C	Y	N	Y	Y	Y	Y	Y	Y	Y		Y	Y
Spokane	186,562	C		N	Y	Y		Y	Y	Y		Y	Y	Y
Tacoma	176,664	C	N	N	Y							Y	Y	Y

State and Jurisdiction	1990 pop.	Type	Contingency plan that covers vital services in the event of a work stoppage	Legal deadline for conclusion of collective bargaining prior to budget submission	Management rights clause in any contracts	Set standards and level of service	Determine procedures and standards of selection for employment and promotion	Take disciplinary action	Relieve employees from duty with cause	Establish shifts as necessary	Determine content of job classifications	Decide whether to contract or subcontract for services	Determine missions, policies, budget, and general operations	Determine size and composition of workforce
Tukwila	14,506	C	N	N	Y	Y	Y	Y	Y	Y	Y		Y	Y
Tumwater	11,520	C	N	N	Y			Y	Y		Y			Y
University Place	32,000	C	Y	N	Y	Y	Y	Y	Y	Y	Y	Y	Y	Y
Vancouver	54,651	C	N	N	Y	Y			Y	Y	Y	Y	Y	Y
Walla Walla	26,478	C	N	N	Y	Y	Y	Y	Y	Y	Y	Y	Y	Y
West Virginia														
Clarksburg	18,059	C	N											
Huntington	54,844	C	Y	N	Y	Y	Y	Y	Y		Y		Y	
Wisconsin														
Allouez	14,431	V	N	N	Y	Y	Y	Y	Y		Y		Y	Y
Appleton	65,695	C	N	N	Y		Y	Y	Y	Y	Y		Y	Y
Beloit	35,573	C	N	N	Y	Y		Y	Y			Y	Y	Y
Brookfield	35,184	C	N	N	Y	Y	Y		Y	Y	Y		Y	Y
De Pere	16,569	C	N	N	Y	Y	Y	Y	Y	Y	Y	Y	Y	Y
Eau Claire	56,856	C	Y	N	Y			Y	Y					
Franklin	21,855	C	Y	N	Y			Y	Y	Y				
Grand Chute	14,490	T	N	N	Y	Y								Y
Greendale	15,128	V	N	N	Y	Y		Y		Y			Y	Y
Janesville	52,133	C	N	N	Y	Y	Y	Y	Y	Y	Y	Y		Y
Kaukauna	11,982	C	N	N	Y									
Menasha	14,711	C	N	N	Y									

State and Jurisdiction	1990 pop.	Type	Contingency plan that covers vital services in the event of a work stoppage	Legal deadline for conclusion of collective bargaining prior to budget submission	Management rights clause in any contracts	Set standards and level of service	Determine procedures and standards of selection for employment and promotion	Take disciplinary action	Relieve employees from duty with cause	Establish shifts as necessary	Determine content of job classifications	Decide whether to contract or subcontract for services	Determine missions, policies, budget, and general operations	Determine size and composition of workforce
Menasha	15,094	T	N	N	Y	Y	Y	Y	Y	Y	Y	Y	Y	Y
Menomonie	13,547	C	N	N	Y		Y	Y	Y	Y	Y	Y		Y
Muskego	16,813	C	Y	N	Y	Y		Y			Y	Y	Y	
Oak Creek	19,513	C	N	N	Y	Y	Y	Y	Y	Y	Y	Y	Y	Y
Onalaska	11,284	C	N	N	Y	Y	Y	Y	Y	Y	Y		Y	Y
Racine	84,298	C	Y	N	Y	Y		Y	Y	Y		Y	Y	Y
Shorewood	14,116	V	N	N	Y	Y	Y	Y	Y	Y	Y		Y	Y
South Milwaukee	20,958	C	N	N	Y		Y	Y	Y	Y	Y	Y		
Stevens Point	23,006	C	N	N	Y	Y	Y	Y				Y		
Sun Prairie	15,333	C	N	N	Y	Y		Y	Y	Y	Y	Y	Y	Y
Superior	27,134	C	N	N	Y	Y	Y	Y	Y	Y	Y	Y	Y	Y
Two Rivers	13,030	C	N	N	Y	Y	Y	Y	Y	Y	Y	Y	Y	
Watertown	19,142	C	N	N	Y	Y	Y	Y	Y	Y	Y		Y	Y
Waukesha	56,958	C	N	N	Y	Y	Y	Y	Y	Y	Y		Y	Y
West Allis	63,221	C	Y	N	Y	Y	Y	Y	Y	Y	Y		Y	Y
West Bend	23,916	C	N	N	Y		Y	Y	Y	Y	Y	Y	Y	Y
Weston	10,863	T	N	N	Y	Y	Y						Y	Y
Whitefish Bay	14,272	V	N	N	N									
Whitewater	12,636	C	N	N	Y	Y	Y	Y	Y	Y	Y	Y	Y	Y

State and Jurisdiction	1990 pop.	Type	Contingency plan that covers vital services in the event of a work stoppage	Legal deadline for conclusion of collective bargaining prior to budget submission	Management rights clause in any contracts	Set standards and level of service	Determine procedures and standards of selection for employment and promotion	Take disciplinary action	Relieve employees from duty with cause	Establish shifts as necessary	Determine content of job classifications	Decide whether to contract or subcontract for services	Determine missions, policies, budget, and general operations	Determine size and composition of workforce
Wisconsin Rapids	18,245	C	N	N	Y	Y	Y	Y	Y	Y	Y	Y	Y	Y
Wyoming														
Casper	46,742	C	N	N	Y	Y	Y	Y	Y	Y	Y		Y	Y
Cheyenne	50,008	C	N	Y	Y									
Laramie	26,687	C	N	Y	Y	Y	Y	Y	Y	Y	Y	Y	Y	Y